Guide for Employees to Rise in Service

S.K. Tarafder

ATLANTIC®
PUBLISHERS & DISTRIBUTORS

Published by

ATLANTIC®

PUBLISHERS & DISTRIBUTORS

B-2, Vishal Enclave, Opp. Rajouri Garden,
New Delhi-110027
Phones : 25413460, 25429987, 25466842

Sales Office
7/22, Ansari Road, Darya Ganj,
New Delhi-110002
Phones : 23273880, 23275880, 23280451
Fax : 91-11-23285873
web : www.atlanticbooks.com
e-mail : info@atlanticbooks.com

Printed in India
at Nice Printing Press, Delhi

Preface

Barring a few, employees are not born officers. Instances are plenty that many non-managerial employees have become managers in well reputable organisations. This has become possible by virtue of their putting in concerted efforts for considerable years. This book is a complete guidance to the employees who have innate inclination to ascend to high position in service at the quickest possible time. Employees working in organisations should bear in mind that promotion in service is not automatic and spontaneous. One who is found fittest is given promotion in service in preference to others, even denying the principle of seniority usually adopted in organisations for awarding promotion to employees. It is quite possible that an employee enjoying seniority in service may be lacking in qualities which are essential for further promotion in service. Therefore, only those employees are considered for promotion, no matter they may be junior to the other employees, who are fully endowed with the qualities needed for working in managerial position. This book has dealt with number of aspects which the employees must adhere to in order to get promotion in service in quick succession.

Needless to elucidate, ambitious employees are the architects of shaping their own future. There is a saying, "As you sow so you reap." Accordingly, the employees will reap the harvest as they sow. For developing their future career, the employees must be enthusiastic and this enthusiasm will generate when they will follow the instructions and guidance as contained in this book. Usually, employees continue to work in organisations in a beaten track for years without knowing how to transform their way of working for prosperity in service. This book is an eye-opener and a torchbearer to the employees to pave their way to rise high in service. Through questions and answers many information has been highlighted which will give extensive knowledge not only to the ambitious aspirants but also to the working employees as well. It is essential that while working in organisations they must keep themselves abreast of such information.

If the instructions and guidance as discussed in this book are followed by the employees with right earnest and seriousness, they are destined to be crowned with success in their service career. Hence, this book is a must for all the employees in their own interest, as it has tremendous educative value.

In this book I have used masculine gender, such as 'He/ Manager' without mentioning the feminine counterpart, such as She/Manageress. I beg apology from the female readers of this book for not mentioning feminine gender, in fact, I have used the masculine gender only for convenience purpose in writing.

S.K. TARAFDER

Contents

Developing Sense of Responsibility

1

A responsible employee is an asset to an Organisation. Responsibility generates out of keenness to do work with seriousness by an employee. A responsible employee is trusted upon for any work entrusted to him. Officers feel complacent with an employee of responsibility. Company's work never suffers when a responsible employee is set to work with aptness. Being responsible an employee is destined to rise in service. When responsibility is involved in every sphere of working of an officer, an employee desiring to ascend to high position must cultivate the sense of responsibility from the very beginning of his service career.

Irresponsible employees are not in any way considered part and parcel of a Company. To all intents and purposes, such employee is a heavy burden to the Organisation where he works. The output of his work is far below the quantum of salary/remuneration he receives from the Company. An irresponsible employee cannot gain confidence of the higher management and his future with the Company is blocked. Such irresponsible employee gives opportunity to the higher management to find faults with his working which results in the insecurity of his services of the Company and at times such employee even loses his job with the Company. The employees who are irresponsible and work carelessly do not have the least intention to prosper in life through service. Such irresponsible employees contaminate the efficient working in the Organisation and there becomes the stumbling block on the part of the Organisation to march forward to prosperity. Attaining prosperity by a Company is the result of efficient and responsible working of the employees collectively.

A responsible employee is endeared by his superior officer/ Manager. Such employee is always dependable. A dependable employee is voracious and fully devoted to his working. When an employee is responsible he can easily win the hearts of his superior officer/Manager. By conquering their hearts being responsible in the performance of duties the position of the employee in the Organisation is cemented and he continues to work with free mind. Working with free mind helps the employee perform job flawless. Such employee doing job to the complete satisfaction of his superior officer/Manager because of perfection in the job done, becomes worry-free. A responsible employee never quarrels with his work because he finds it easy to accomplish even the difficult job entrusted to him.

Responsibility in the working of an employee is the yard-stick of his prosperity in service. There are ways as to how an employee can develop sense of responsibility in his working which are discussed as under:

(a) Employees must have propensity to work with sincerity.

(b) Company's work to be done by the employees has to be treated as their own work.

(c) Employees must have fondness to the Company whole-heartedly and then only sense of responsibility in the working will be infused in the minds of the employees.

(d) Employees must have desire to ascend to high position in service which will be possible when they are responsible to their working.

(e) Employees should get themselves endeared with the high officials and their encouragement in the performance of work will generate sense of responsibility to the employees.

When an employee is responsible in the discharge of his duties, his mind is fully devoted to the working always and he does not feel pleasure to while away time in the office leaving aside the work. Full devotion to work with responsibility freshens his mind also and he gets impetus to work. By his responsibility he feels that work is worship. Other employees who are not responsible to the desired level are also inspired to boost up their responsibility at the instance of the employees who are fully responsible in their working. Needless to emphasise, developing sense of responsibility in the performance of duties is an essential ingredient on the part of an employee to succeed in the field of employment.

Punctuality in Attendance to Office without becoming a Clock Watcher | 2

An employee must be punctual in attendance to office. His devotion to duties is reflected through punctuality. Without devotion to duties an employee cannot think of rising high in service. A sincere employee must be disciplined. Punctuality breeds discipline. Discipline is the mother of success. Indisciplined and haphazard way of working cannot bring perfection in working. Without perfection in working Company's work suffers a lot and the employee proves himself inefficient. Inefficiency in the working of an employee tells upon his prosperity in service. An organisation becomes prosperous when employees maintain punctuality in attendance to office. When an organisation is prosperous the future of the employees is also prosperous. Employees should bear in mind that with the growth of the Company they have also to grow.

Employees' contribution for the growth of the organisation is immense. Punctuality in attendance which brings discipline is the key to success of an employee in the organisation. Punctuality in attendance by an employee is indicative of his voracity and love for work which augurs well for his future prosperity in service. Disciplined way of working increases efficiency of an employee. The employee who is efficient can only think of rise in service, because the speciality in the knowledge required for working in high position is the sequence of efficient working which is correlated with maintaining punctuality in attendance to duties.

Habitual impunctuality in the attendance to duties by an employee demonstrates that he has no love for work in the office. Such an employee is most unreliable and axes on his own feet in his future career. Such an employee also spoils the punctuality in attendance of other employees who are apt to follow suit of other impunctual employees and the discipline of the organisation as a whole is impaired. Progress of employees is halted when the organisation runs through indiscipline which holds the onus of responsibility of impunctual attendance to duties by the employees. When impunctual attendance to duties of the employees at large results in the debilitation of the Company, the future of the employees are shadowed about which the employees must be aware of. No employee should, therefore, indulge in impunctual attendance to duties in their own interest.

In the office there is no limit to work. When it is a known fact that prosperity of a person is attained in the wake of devotion to work, which has no time limit, the employees must not be clock watchers to leave the office at the very nick of time leaving the work half done. Leaving the office just at the appointed time of office hours does not indicate that the duties of the employees have been completed for the day. The employees aspiring to rise high in service must have to take the instance of the officers/Managers still working late hours, as they are very much conscious of the working of the organisation. The employees have also to engage themselves fully to the working of the organisation in their own interest being oblivious of the time limit. Such a tendency of the employees combining the working of the Company in their lives with full devotion and without time limit will pave the way for their future prosperity in the organisation.

It is strongly recommended that the employees must inculcate the habit of punctual attendance to office at any cost doing away with the tendency of leaving the office just at the nick of time of office hours, if they really aspire to rise high in service. In this connection, it will not be out of place to mention here that the employees forming union in an establishment do not want to overstay in the office as they believe in working clinging strictly to the timing of office hours. Such employees bother least whether the work has been completed or not before they leave the office for the day. They should not leave the half done work to be completed next day. While formation of Union in an establishment is a matter of right of the employees and that there is no taboo for formation of the same under any legislation, it is not of course the principle of the Union that the employees should vacate the office punctually after days work — no matter the work of the organisation has been completed or not. The employees must bear in mind that formation of Union has nothing to do with their sincere working for the organisation even by over-staying in the office in their own interest.

Not to Waste Time in Office Chit-chatting with other Employees Keeping the Work in Arrear

3

Office is not a rendezvous. But it is a place for working by the employees in unison with full devotion and sincerity. Every employee has allotted work and he is held responsible for accomplishing the same to the entire satisfaction of his superior officer/Manager. Slackness in the discharge of his official duties is an indication that he is a nagging employee, which proves of his disqualification. This does not augur well for his future prosperity. Such an employee cannot be in the good books of his superior officer/Manager and this leads to blockade of his future career in the organisation.

Habit of wastage of time by an employee leaving the work incomplete speaks of his laziness and insincerity. A lazy and insincere employee cannot rise in high position. The output of work of a lazy employee is very low and the work allotted to him goes on piling up everyday and ultimately he feels perplexed and fish out of water, when he finds heaps of work before him. In such circumstances, there is no alternative for him but to think of leaving the employment, as he starts perceiving that such an inefficient employee like him has no place in the organisation. Also his peace of mind is robbed of and he continues to suffer from extreme tension.

As an employee habit of gossiping during working hours leaving his work incomplete shows that he is not a disciplined employee. An indisciplined employee is a misfit in an organisation. Such employee disturbs the working of other employees also whose efficiency is dwindled as a result of coming in contact with such indisciplined employee and the organisational discipline as a whole is impaired. No organisation can ill afford to run with the nagging employees who are not interested in putting in seriousness of working but find pleasure in wasting time leaving the work to the care of none.

An employee who is actually very serious in rising high in service never thinks of wasting time leaving the work incomplete and also keeping the same in arrear which goes on piling up everyday. Such employee leaves a good impression in the minds of his senior officer/Manager that he is worthy of shouldering higher responsibilities, as he is competent to work with perfection without keeping the work in arrear. Employees working with devotion and sincerity are the assets of an organisation and such employees are actually the pillars of an organisation and their case is considered favourably by the higher management for placing them to work in high position. The employees who are lazy and are in the habit of whiling away precious time in the office in gossiping and keeping the work in arrear have in fact no right to work in the organisation and receive salaries.

No employee should think that his ambition has been fulfilled after getting employment. But, he has yet to go a long way in thriving through employment. For this, he is to be ambitious and his ambition will be crowned with success when he is fully devoted to work without wasting time unnecessarily. By keeping the work up-to-date he will feel relieved of his responsibilities and this relief will keep him cheerful and he will be fully magnetised to work in the office. A sincere employee should think that he is inalienable from office with perception that work is worship.

To sum up, an employee with full devotion to work without whiling away time in the office and keeping the work in arrear is destined to rise high in service and such employee working in high position will be found dependable in the eyes of the higher management. Interaction with the higher management by a senior officer/Manager is essentially needed for enjoying his exalted position in the organisation. Employees should, therefore, work with full devotion for their prosperity thus enabling them to maintain rapprochement/and interaction with the higher management. The devoted employees will get sympathies always from the higher officials in times of any predicament.

Not to Get Ill-tempered to See the Spate of Work | 4

An employee desiring to rise in service holding responsible position as an officer/Manager ought to know that he has to pass through spate of work and under no circumstances he should be ruffled in temperament in dealing with such volumes of work. If he gets ill-tempered and ruffled to see the spate of work to be done by him, it will be a distant dream for him to ascend to high position in service. Patience is a great virtue and a moral excellence by dint of which an employee can excel in dealing with voluminous work with calm and ease. Keeping normalcy in his temperament in dealing with the spate of work is very important which is essentially needed to work with efficiency and this efficiency in working is the stepping stone for an employee to rise in service.

As an employee he must get trained up from the very beginning of his working as an Assistant and the like in adjusting himself with the spate of work in view of the fact that he will be required to deal with the volumes of work as an officer of the company when promoted so that he can have plain sailing in dealing with such voluminous work without being ruffled.

An employee must be aware of that the function of an officer/Manager is multifarious and not conventionalised. His mind has to play in different ways in dealing with different nature of work and that too with maturity of thought. Maturity of thought is acquired through unruffled temperament. With cool brain and normal state of mind a successful officer/ Manager can sort out the intricacies of problems. He will stumble at every stage if he becomes choleric in disposition in dealing with spate of work. One important point is that keeping normalcy in dealing with volumes of work, an officer/ Manager is essentially needed to be humorous and jovial which will exterminate his unsteady state of mind and he will feel easy to deal with even the most complicated work. If an officer/Manager is irked to find the volumes of work, disposal of the same will be procrastinated with the result that there will be continuous piling of work and it will go out of his capacity and control to deal with such voluminous work.

An employee being aware of the working of a successful officer/Manager as discussed in the foregoing, should start getting prepared to work in the like manner, for which maintaining cool temperament in dealing with spate of work is essential right from the beginning of his working as an employee/Assistant. The patience of the employee in dealing with the volumes of work will naturally attract the attention of his immediate superior officer/Manager.

The following are the ways as to how an employee can remain unruffled while dealing with the spate of work:

(a) While working the employee has to remain free from scarce and anxieties.

(b) He must have pleasing disposition with cool temperament and remain jovial.

(c) He will have to work with free mind.

(d) He should think that the work he is doing is his own work.

(e) He should give a bit pause in dealing with the voluminous work. Otherwise, he will feel fatigue.

(f) During the course of dealing with the spate of work he should not be irksome with the other co-employees. Also he should show tenderness while talking to the officer/Manager.

To sum up, an employee's future in the organisation will blossom if he can conquer ruffled temperament while dealing with the volumes of work by following the guidelines, as enumerated above. Whatever may be the situation in the office, employees must have endurance to deal with the spate of work in normal state of mind without getting choleric in disposition and here lies their greatness as employees thus paving the way for their advancement in future. Man has come down to the world to work and hence he must not be apprehensive of spate of work. This should also be the watch word of the employees to rise high in service.

An Employee should Gain Confidence of the Senior Officers/Managers

5

Officers/Managers should be the confidants of the higher management. Otherwise, it will be meaningless to work in such capacity. They have to deal with many confidential matters and if these things are leaked out through them, the higher management will be put to trying position which will be detrimental to the interest of the organization. Hence, the Company's image is intimately related to the workings of the officers/Managers. If they are not relied upon in the discharge of their duties, they are considered snakes in the grass and they are not competent to work officers/Managers of the Organisation. In such case, their services with the organisation are also at stake. Faithfulness of officers/Managers is essentially needed to gain/confidence of the higher management. But, at the same time, this faithfulness must not be spiced with oily tongue. In fact, the higher management must be fully complacent with the officers/Managers after they are saddled with any confidential and/or non-confidential jobs to be performed by them to their entire satisfaction and with confidence.

The foregoing is the explanation in respect of the absolute necessity that the employees who have innate desire to work as officers/Managers in due course of time during the course of their employment must infuse in them that they are also confidants of the senior officers/Managers under whom they have been working.

An employee without having confidence of the management cannot think of ascending high in service. It is imperative that when an employee enters the threshold of service he must think of winning confidence of the management by the discharge of his loyal and sincere services. Sincerity and loyalty bread confidence and this confidence leads the employee to shoulder higher responsibilities. Infusing confidence in the minds of the management with sincerity in job makes an employee result oriented and he must be rewarded with higher responsibilities.

Many employees have a wrong conception that giving vent to confidential matters of the organisation to their co-employees/ colleagues, if the same per chance come to their knowledge, speaks high of them in the eyes of other employees. Such employees feel pleasure that the other employees put them in high esteem as they are in the know of many confidential matters of the organization. This notion is pernicious. This exhibits their light heartedness which is a retrograde step to rise high in service. An employee must be reserved, so that the attempts of other employees are not made successful to extract from him the confidential matters of the organisation.

The employees who have the absolute desire to rise in service must cultivate as to how confidence could be instilled in the minds of the senior officers/Managers of the Company and the ways of building the same are as follows:

(a) While working in office with other colleagues he must maintain reservation, so that the other employees bear in mind that no confidential matter of the company could be extracted from him.

(b) It must be borne in mind by the employee that leakage of confidential matters would be disastrous for the organisation and that the preservation of confidential matters by him will speak high of him.

(c) The employee who is fickle minded cannot preserve confidential matters. It is, therefore, of utmost necessity that he should have solemnity.

(d) The employee who is taciturn is the person of confidence having maintained confidential matters. Therefore, he must practise taciturnity to gain confidence of the management.

To conclude, the employee desiring to ascend to high position must create confidence in the minds of the management by abiding by the guidance, as enumerated above. It is to be borne in mind by the employee that leakage of confidential matters through him will shatter confidence in him by the management and once the confidence is lost, it cannot be regained and that his image in the organisation will be slandered and he will be put to precarious position — what to talk of his advancement in the organisation.

Need to Develop Personality | 6

Personality counts much on the part of an employee to ascend to exalted position in service. Respectability of a person comes through personality. A person without personality is not esteemed. Through personality many impracticable things can be got accomplished. Officers of a company ought to be the persons endowed with personalities. With their personalities they command respects from the employees and also they are esteemed everywhere. Personality is an essential ingredient which the employees have to cultivate in the interest of their rising high in service career during the course of employment. Personality does not mean that a person is essentially required to be good looking. Appearance and other factors are considered to determine personality of an employee. In fact, personality cult of an employee depicts the following:

(1) Self-confidence.

(2) Fixity of mind.

(3) Capacity to influence others.

(4) Clarity of expression.

(5) Not to be fickle minded.

(6) Capacity of quick understanding of things.

(7) Wearing of well fitted costumes. Shoes he puts on should be polished.

(8) Positive approach on matters.

(9) Cleanliness.

(10) Gravity.

(11) Proper dressing of hair. He must have daily shaving of face. But, this will not apply to those keeping beard.

(12) Steadiness in walking.

(13) Sense of etiquette.
(14) Good manners.
(15) Will power.
(16) Gentleness.
(17) Good behaviour.
(18) Deportment.
(19) Soft spoken.
(20) Cool temperament.
(21) Loveable habits.
(22) Strait forwardness.

Embodiment of the qualities in an employee, as enumerated above, is an index of pleasing personality which is very important to ascend to high, position in service as also attain all-round success in life. It is, therefore, absolutely necessary that an employee coveting to ascend to lofty position in service should inculcate the above traits by regular systematic practice.

Conception of a few of the employees that they are not good looking and hence it will be impracticable on their part to practise the traits of personality, as mentioned above, is absolutely wrong. They should bear in mind that personality is something which helps change the characteristics of a person altogether. It will not be incongruous to mention in this connexion that even a good looking person is devoid of personality if he does not possess the above traits of personality. Personality makes a man perfect and people around him gravitate towards him as also in the case of employees working in office.

To conclude, needless to emphasise, personality of an employee is the stepping stone for attaining prosperity in service. An employee possessing personality is an asset to the Organisation where he is employed and the Organisation is also proud of having such employee on its role. Personality is something which is to be cultivated. It is not spontaneous. A few of the employees are of the impression that with position personality comes automatically. This conception of theirs is not correct. If an employee is destitute of personality during the course of his working as Assistant or the like, on what basis could he expect to ascend to the ladder of prosperity in service. Hence, personality has to be practised from the early stages before he starts working in managerial position. Success in the working of a senior officer/Manager is attained through personality. Personality plays a very important role in the field of employment. Employees who are ambitious of ascending to the high position must take care of cultivating personality.

Dealings with Other Employees of the Company | 7

An officer/Manager after getting promotion has to work in conglomeration with the employees and getting their cooperation is of paramount necessity to prove himself that he is worthy of elevated position. Even if an officer is efficient in the discharge of his duties by virtue of his matured thoughts and ideas, he will stumble to prove his efficiency when the employees with whom he worked before his promotion will be showing their non-cooperative attitude towards him. It is the practice with a few of the promoted officers/Managers that during the course of their working as Assistants or the like their dealings with the co-employees were quite sweet, cordial and harmonious but after they have ascended to high position their dealings with the employees start changing with the notion that they are superior to them in all respects. This change of attitude should not be truly in the fitness of things on the part of the promoted employees. Change of dealings after getting promotion would not speak high of them and there will be question mark about their competence holding high position. Without cooperation of the employees an officer/Manager will be put to difficult situation, because the organisational work is carried on with the united efforts of the employees and the officers/Managers. Employees aspiring for high position should, therefore, take instance from the above about the importance of maintaining cordial relations with the co-employees always.

Dealings of an employee with the high officials as also with the co-employees in soothing and courteous manner speak high of him. This shows that he has hailed from a family of respectability. Needless to elucidate, such an employee enjoys respects from all and sundry in the organisation and gets all sorts of cooperation in his working. This in turn helps him work with complete peace of mind and consequently develops his working spirit which is a prerequisite to pave the way to attain prosperity in service. Talking in unbecoming way irks other employees as also the officers and he cannot win their hearts. This is no doubt one of the shortcomings of such an employee which stands in the way of his rising high in service.

Decent and courteous dealings of an employee pay him in other ways also. While doing job outside on behalf of the organisation, he can implant a good impression in the minds of the officials of other organisations by his courteous dealings and he can be crowned with success in getting the job done to the advantage of his parent Company. This is his additional attainment as an employee which pays him in the long run. The higher management attaches high hopes on such employee which benefits him in the long run.

An employee dealing nicely is loveable by all. He can adjust with any situation that may crop up. He never becomes a misfit with any Organisation he serves and he feels homely with the Organisation. His co-employees come forward with helping hands whenever he feels difficulty in doing any job entrusted to him. This is purely on account of his maintaining cordial relations with them by his courteous dealings. His officer/Manager is also proud of having such employee working under him. An employee with courteous dealings quickens his pace to rise high in service.

From what has been discussed in the foregoing, it has transpired that an employee desiring to rise high in service must be courteous in dealings with all his co-employees and officers/Managers and at no point of time he should exhibit his ruffled temperament. It is a known fact that an employee with courteous and soothing behaviour is a person of cool temperament which is absolutely necessary on the part of an employee to shoulder higher responsibilities with calm and ease. Such an employee will never feel irritated when he is saddled with voluminous work and the work of the

Organisation will be accomplished systematically and in apple-pie order. An employee must have, therefore, cool temperament which is the result of courteous and soothing behaviour with all in order to pave his way glossy for higher position.

8 Trustworthiness

An employee must be trustworthy in his actions, behaviour and character. It is of utmost necessity that he has to maintain good rapprochement with his senior officer/Manager and also with his co-employees and this rapprochement should be based on trust. The working of an employee without interaction and/or rapprochement and trust will be void and he cannot be taken into confidence by the higher management. Without this confidence the employee will be practically isolated from his senior officer/Manager and this isolation will be a stumbling block to rise high in service. During the course of working, building trust and confidence by an employee is very important. The crux of the question is how to build trust. The factors for building trust are as follows:

(a) The employee has to build confidence by his sincerity and honesty of working.

(b) He must have unblemished character.

(c) He should give due respect to his senior officer/ Manager under whom he is working.

(d) He must have consistency between his words and deeds.

(e) He must prove his competence and attitude to service.

(f) He must be a person of integrity.

(g) He must create impression that he is a person of reliability.

(h) He must not be a flatterer.

(i) Truthfulness is another virtue of creating trust.

If an employee loses confidence in his senior officer/ Manager, he cannot enjoy the laurels of his position and that he will always be a suspicious person, which will be detrimental to his interest in the working of the Organisation and this will be a retrograde step in his service career. He will be considered unworthy of the services of the Company and the higher management will think of getting rid of such employee losing trust and confidence.

An employee ought to know that following are the factors which breed distrust:

(a) Negative attitude.

(b) Lack of courtesy.

(c) Inconsistent and uncooperative deportment and behaviour.

(d) Lack of honesty and integrity.

(e) Selfishness.

Trust without integrity cannot be generated. An employee has to nurture the notion always that the trust he has created remains perpetual, as this will pave the way for rise in his service career. He should bear in mind that without creating trust and confidence in the minds of his senior officer/Manager as also in the higher management his working in the Organisation will have no meaning and rise in his service will have a blockade.

It has been observed that in many cases employees are working in the Organisation without seriousness, as they are under the impression that they cannot think of rising high in service. This is a wrong conception. They must have the notion that man is the architect of his own fate and in the field of employment an employee is the architect of building his own position after he creates trust and confidence by his sincere working, in the minds of his senior officer/Manager and also the higher management. Employees should also bear in mind that their success in employment for working in high position may take a few years' time and that they must not feel despondent and dejected, as the fortune and prosperity of a person does not come by surprise but by sincere endeavour with trust and confidence.

From what has been discussed in the foregoing in respect of building trustworthiness and confidence, it has transpired that the future of the employees depends upon how far they have been able to create confidence and trust in the minds of the management, and in this connection the employees should follow the guidelines, as mentioned from serial nos. (a) to (e), with right earnest. No employee should feel dejected that his fortune will not smile. His future is in his own hands. Creating trust in the minds of the management is very important in order to create position in the Organisation and the employees should not be lacking in it.

Intelligence | 9

Needless to emphasise, intelligence is an indispensable qualification of an employee which will help him rise in exalted position in service, because for working in managerial position intelligence is a prerequisite, as by virtue of intelligent decisions taken in matters of insurmountable problems facing any organisation a Manager paves his way to come in the limelight as a magnetic force in the eyes of the higher management and his prospect in the Organisation is enlarged. An intelligent employee has quick grasping capacity of things and by dint of his grasping capacity his knowledge of working in the Organisation is deepened at the quickest possible time. This broadens his opportunity to ascend to higher position in service.

An intelligent employee is a solid pillar in an Organisation. Such employee has quick analytical capacity to thrash out any complicated work that may be faced by him and solve problems. This chapter will be incomplete if it is not discussed how intelligence of an employee could be developed. It is of course an admitted fact that intelligence of an employee has its own originality. But, still then it could be developed further by the under-mentioned methods which are analysed seriatim:

(a) Employees must have mental acumen to come to a definite conclusion after analysing the facts and circumstances of matters.

(b) Mixing up with different strata of people to know about their views of variegated nature and then analysing the correctness of the same by exercising the original power of brain. This will develop intelligent quotient (I.Q.) of the employees.

(c) Coming in contact with the galaxy of intellectuals to know about their perception of things.

(d) By way of gleaning practical experience.

(e) Propensity to know the unknown.

(f) Contemplation on any matter seriously to know about its merits and demerits.

(g) Brain should not be kept idle and thinking power should be made stronger.

(h) Should be very much voracious to observe how the senior officer/Manager takes decisions under different situations and by this way mental faculty of the employee could be developed.

If all these are practised there will be broadening of mental faculties thereby developing intelligence of an employee.

Without intelligence and sharpness of mind an employee cannot shoulder higher responsibilities. Working in higher position means that he has to take many decisions instantly and these decisions must have reactions, as every action has reaction. Therefore, when taking decisions is closely connected with intelligence quotient, the employees preparing for ascending to higher position must practise developing intelligence by adhering to the above methods.

Employees have to remember always that intelligence is a very important factor to work successfully in higher position. Otherwise, there will be every possibility that they will falter at every stage while going for taking decisions in the capacity of senior officer/Manager. Intelligent employees contribute perfection in the discharge of their duties and the Organisations are benefitted by the working of such intelligent employees. Development and expansion of Organisations are quick when there are galaxy of intellectual employees working combinedly. Intelligent employees never lag behind and they have to be rewarded by way of promotion in higher position. No enlightened Organisation ignores intelligent employees because such employees are assets to them and their elevation to exalted position is inevitable.

It is imperative that the higher management should groom up the intelligent employees by giving them necessary training in different aspects. By this, the employees will also feel elated and exhibit their intelligence in a more pragmatic way which in turn will be advantageous for the Organisation. Intelligent working of the employees is always desirable as its benefits are far-reaching.

Attitude of an Employee | 10

Positive attitude of an employee contributes to success. It applies to every sphere of life including one's personal and professional life. An employee cannot win success in his endeavour to rise in higher position in service, if he has negative attitude. His senior officer/Manager finds difficulty in dealing with such employee and when he is not happy with him the future of the employee in the Organisation cannot be promising. An employee with positive attitude is like a fruit of all seasons. An employee with positive attitude gets cooperation of all which is essentially needed for his systematic way of working in the Organisation. He has to remember that without cooperation of others his working cannot be free from flaws in all cases. He wins confidence of his senior officer/Manager through perfection of working which is possible when he has positive attitude.

An employee should always bear in mind that negative attitude breeds bitterness and resentment in the minds of his senior officer/Manager and his co-employees. Negative attitude of an employee negates organised working in the office. Therefore, an employee must abjure negative attitude in the interest of attaining success in the field of his profession. An employee with negative attitude never reconciles with reasonings of others and sticks to his own one-sided opinion only without any reason which is not usually acceptable to others. For his negative attitude he is always in tussle with his co-employees which does not augur well for him. Also an employee without positive attitude does not want to learn things from others which results in limiting his working knowledge. Such employee with negative attitude is a misfit in an Organisation and cannot prosper in life.

An employee ought to be in the know that positive attitude has the undermentioned advantages:

(a) Fosters team work in the Organisation which helps the employees increase their working efficiency.

(b) Improves quality of work.

(c) Fosters better relations with the co-employees and senior officer/Manager.

(d) Creates congenial atmosphere in the office.

(e) Generates loyalty in the minds of the employees.

(f) Helps solve problems.

(g) Ensures cooperative attitude amongst employees.

In this connexion, it is appropriate to mention as to how to develop positive attitude, if an employee is devoid of the same:

(a) Beware of the principles that builds a positive attitude.

(b) Desire to be positive.

(c) Cultivate discipline and dedication.

(d) Have refined temperament.

(e) Be well-mannered and soft minded.

From the analyses as elucidated in the foregoing, it comes out crystal clear that stiff attitude of an employee negates him to ascend to high position in service. Such employee is a liability for an Organisation. It is, therefore, absolutely necessary that the employee who has innate desire to rise high in service, must abjure negative attitude. An employee with positive attitude is endeared by all and gets all sorts of cooperation in the discharge of his duties whenever he finds difficulty in doing any complicated work. Such employee also learns things quickly which hastens his future prosperity in the Organisation. His senior officer/Manager too has a soft corner in his mind for such an employee with positive attitude. He never creates problems on any issue because he is not an employee of contradiction.

It is advisable that when an employee becomes a senior officer/Manager he must not develop negative attitude, else he will be detrimental to his position. Negative attitude is a great disqualification on the part of a promising employee. An employee with positive attitude is always amenable to the reasoning of the higher management with humility.

An Employee is to be Hard-working | 11

Nothing is impracticable without strenuous labour. A person is crowned with success in his every endeavour when he puts in hard labour. Man rises to prominence and high position by virtue of his vigorous work. Industry is the mother of success. Today is the age of cut-throat competition and survival of the fittest, which is attained by dint of hard work. There is no substitution for hard work. Idling away time brings misery and misfortune. Prosperity and self-development of a person are achieved through hard work only. In service career also employees climb to high position by strenuous labour. One cannot develop a capacity to do anything without hard work. "The harder you work the luckier you get"—says Henry Ford. Success of a person does not come by accident. Everything that we enjoy is the result of hard work. Hard work makes a person better at whatever he is doing. Great talent without will-power and hard work is a waste. There is no magic wand for success. Excellence is not luck; it is the result of a lot of hard work and practice.

It is now amply clear that when hard work is the panacea for attaining success in life, an employee doing hard work in the office is destined to climb to the top of the ladder of success. There are ample evidences that employees from the very humble positions have risen to high positions and the secrecy of the same is their putting in hard work. The employee who is afraid of hard work and/or detracts from the same is a failure in life and can never rise to high position. A hard working employee is a very happy person and feels cosy of his duties because the work which he is entrusted to do never gets piled up. Accumulation of work is caused by easy going habits of the employee, for which he feels mentally disturbed and tormented and, therefore, cannot do justice to the Organisation through his work. Such an employees is always irresponsible and cannot be relied upon by his superior officer/Manager.

An employee can make things easy when he has mastered the fundamentals of hard work. When he is accustomed with hard work he is oblivious of what is idle time and leisure time. The harder an employee works, the better he feels; and the better he feels, the harder he works. In the real world, success comes to doers and not to the observers. Hence, success of an employee depends upon how much time he puts in doing hard work.

A hard working employee can consolidate his position at the quickest possible time. Consolidation of position by an employee in an Organisation is an essential prerequisite to rise high in service. Such an employee is dependable in the eyes of the higher management. When an employee is found dependable his rise in service is not a hurdle. A hard working employee is always voracious to mingle with work intimately, as he has the conception that work is worship. This perception of the hard working employee helps him attain exalted position, as he knows that success of a person comes through hard work.

Hard working employees are by far the assets of Organisations. Managements of Organisations can ill-afford to part with the hard working employees. They are retained at any cost. Development and prosperity of Organisations depend largely upon the hard working employees and accordingly with the growth of the Organisations the hard working employees have also the simultaneous growth in their position. Every ambitious employee should, therefore, be hard working for their prosperity in service and live happily without economic morbidity. Hard working employees never feel lethargic and work with enthusiasm. Without hard work efficiency cannot increase. Since the senior officer/Manager is saddled with voluminous work requiring hard work, the employees are also to be hard working so that when they will work in senior position they will not feel irritated in dealing with spate of work.

Hard working employees never falter in their life-time. Work gravitates them. They are not afraid of hard work rather feel pleasure in doing the same. For them work knows no bounds of timing. They are enlivened through hard work. Organisation guarantees elevation in service rendered by the hard working employees.

Promptness in Working | 12

Promptness in working increases efficiency of employees. Efficient employees have always bright prospects in service. The employee who has easy going habits takes longer time to complete work as a result of which work goes on piling up and he feels fish out of water in dealing with the work entrusted to him. On account of lack of promptness in working he is rendered inefficient and this inefficiency tells upon him heavily in his service career. Such employee having no mind of promptness in working likes very much to while away time having no seriousness in working. He does not have any respects for others also.

Today is the age of speed. Everywhere there is speed and speed. There is no place for the lazy people. Survival of the fittest is the order of the day. Fittest persons are those who are prompt in their working. Through speed and promptness of work an employee can do justice to the Organisation by his output of work. Usefulness of an employee is determined when his work is not kept pending which is possible by the promptness in his working. Devotion to work by an employee results in promptness of work. When an employee starts doing work in the office he should be a person of absolute seriousness. His feelings will be that he has come to work and not to spend time with his co-employees as a get-together in the office.

Efficiency in the working of senior officer/Manager is directly linked with the efficient working with promptness of his staff members, because the work in the department is carried on in unison and not by an individual for collective work. The senior officer/Manager has to depend upon his staff members in many respects and promptness in their working goes a long way in accomplishing the work to the complete satisfaction of the higher management. When the senior officer/

Manager has full satisfaction with his staff members for their promptness and efficient working, it paves the way to rise high in service by such employees. The employees have to appease their immediate boss not by flattery but by promptness and efficient working, because they have the direct link with him in matters of work. The employees have to ensure that no ill-feeling takes root in the minds of their immediate superior officer/Manager towards them. If it is generated for any reason it will be a retrogration for the employees, as it is the senior officer/Manager who recommends to the higher management for their promotion in service.

Promptness in working by the employees can be attained by the practice of the following methods:

(a) Employees must be serious in working.

(b) There should be full concentration of mind while at work.

(c) Employees have to ensure that the work they have started to do is completed at one go and not on piece-meal basis.

(d) They should not indulge in loose talks with other co-employees.

(e) Employees should have the notion that the work they do is their own and not that they are doing the work in lieu of money which they get by way of salary.

(f) Employees should bear in mind that their senior officer/Manager could ask them whether the job entrusted to them has been completed within the reasonable time or not. With such impression the employees will have to speed up the working.

By the above methods followed by the employees promptness in working is bound to come which in consequence efficiency in the working will be attained and it will pave the way in ascending to high position in service by the employees. Promptness in working will also keep the employees felicitous as they will feel free from cumbrousness in dealing with spate of work and their efficiency will go on mounting up by leaps and bounds. All employees should bear in mind that efficient working which results in promptness in dealing with things is extremely important in the field of service. Otherwise, their services with the Organisation may be at stake.

Ensuring Discipline and Maintenance of Cleanliness by Wearing Well-fitted Costumes | 13

Instances are plenty that many talented persons have not been crowned with success in their lives because of their clinging to indiscipline. They have not tried to realise that their failures to attain success were on account of their leading lives of recklessness and in indisciplined way. Haphazard way of working is not discipline. Discipline is a regulated and systematic way of doing things. Peace and happiness of a person comes when he is disciplined. Practice of discipline helps a person reach the desired goal. Discipline is the barometer for progress of human beings. Human life is very much complex and hence easy and peaceful life is conspicuous by its absence in most of the cases. Disciplined way of working is the only answer to bringing peace, happiness and regulated life. Therefore, discipline is very important for every human life.

Having discussed the importance of discipline in the foregoing, it is of absolute necessity that an employee who is ambitious of elevating to high position is required to be disciplined. Otherwise, the work with which he is entrusted with will be in complete disarray. In order to work in managerial capacity an employee has to enforce discipline. When the employee will work as senior officer/Manager, he will be required to maintain strong administration in his department and he will be successful in maintaining the administration only when discipline pervades in his jurisdiction. An employee desiring to work in managerial capacity must be in the know that in absence of maintenance of discipline by a Manager, the employees working under him will be obstinate, reckless and uncontrollable which will be pernicious for the Organisation. Also when discipline is impaired lawlessness prevails everywhere and the Organisation crumbles into economic degeneration and ultimately it is threatened with closure. Maintenance of discipline brings prosperity to an Organisation.

Disciplined way of working is the answer to attaining efficiency by an employee and when he is efficient it is his responsibility to see that discipline is upheld. When attaining efficiency is the result of maintaining discipline by an employee, he is sure to ascend to high position in the Organisation by virtue of being an efficient employee. It is, therefore, of absolute necessity that employees must be disciplined in their own interest. Disciplined employees are assets to Organisation. Discipline constitutes the following:

(a) An employee must be regular and punctual in attendance to office. Punctuality and regularity in attendance to office reflect his attachment to work which expedites attaining working efficiency.

(b) An employee has not to leave his work place abondoning the work and engage himself in unwanted and irrelevant talks with his co-employees thus wasting time for both.

(c) An employee should be polished in talking with his co-employees and senior officers/Managers and pay due respects to their official positions.

(d) When office is not a rendezvous, employees should not resort to talking in loud voice thus disturbing the working of other employees.

(e) An employee should not stroll in the office leaving his work and go outside on some pretext or the other.

(f) An employee should be serious in his working and maintain solemnity.

(g) An employee has to see that through discipline work is kept up-to-date.

Maintenance of cleanliness, wearing well-fitted costumes

Office decorum is very important. Wearing well-fitted and neat and clean costumes by the employees is a part of maintaining office decorum. Employees should wear dress of good taste. It is not compulsory that the employees should come to office wearing costly dress since many of them may not of course afford to buy costly dress. They should, however, wear clean as well as well-fitted and well-creased dress. By wearing dress with pink of perfection an employee presents himself a person of personality, which speaks well of him in the eyes of the higher management. Smartness of an employee is an important factor for his efficient working and he looks smart when he is clad in clean and well-fitted clothes. Wearing graceful dress by an employee has tremendous impact in the business Organisation and the Company's image through the employees wearing neat and well-fitted clothes is enhanced. Such employees can draw attraction of the higher management, which pays them in the long run.

14 Employees should Avail of Minimum Number of Days of Prescribed Leave

It should be the perception of the sincere and loyal employees that they have to prosper in their service career through work. Work knows no bounds. The employees who are shy of work is insincere in every effort and cannot do justice to the fulfilment of their aspirations in life. Man rises to prominence through work. All the persons of the world who have become great dedicated their lives to the tasks before them and they had to work ceaselessly. Perfection in the work comes through hard work. There is a close affinity between man and work. Man should not think of isolating himself from work. He proves justice to his existence when he works. Idle persons are unproductive and they are parasites of the families they belong, the society and the nation as a whole. Such persons have no dream to prosper in life. They are a complete waste. Idle man is susceptible to ailments which weakens them physically. Longevity of life of a man increases when his motto is work. Man rises in life through work only. Through work mind of man remains fresh and with this freshness of mind he can continue to work with vigour and energy. People of both oriental and occidental countries have been working very hard which has resulted in their prosperity. They enjoy life to the brim because they have become prosperous by virtue of work.

In view of what has been narrated above, sincere and dedicated employees should try to avoid clinging to availing of all categories of prescribed leave, so that they can work more which will bring them prosperity. They should think of availing of leave on ground of exigency of situation only and not with the purpose that when there is prescribed leave they should avail of the same entirely even if the situation does not warrant. The prime importance of the employees should be to work sincerely for which they have been appointed. Most of the employees who have risen to high position in service dedicated themselves to the work. For them work is worship. Prosperity in service cannot come without laborious work. The employees who have availed of bare minimum of prescribed leave show how sincere and dedicated they are towards their work.

Sincere and dedicated employees always enjoy upper hand in service in the eyes of the higher management. Such employees have close affinity with them and this paves the way of their future prosperity. In many cases it has been seen that for the high ranking employees holidays are not a bar to them to work in the office. On many holidays they go to office and go on working without clinging to time. Employees aspiring for high position should also take instance from them as to how they devote themselves to work. Employees should bear in mind that work is a pleasure to them and this pleasure will keep them healthy and fresh which will rejuvenate them to work with zeal and vigorous activity. Man has come down to the world to work and not to squander time. There is no dearth of work in this vale of tears. The more man works the more he gains prominence in life.

The main aspect of human beings is work. Persons in employment are fortunate because they get opportunity to work. But, their work should not be linked up with the availing of different categories of leave entirely prescribed in Organisations. Availing of leave is of course necessary for the employees especially when the situation warrants to avail of the same. Organisations have never urged the employees to avail of the entire categories of leave compulsorily. Employees availing of bare minimum of leave gain sympathy of their senior officers/Managers. System of casual leave is there in every Organisation. It is the tendency of the employees to avail of the entire number of days of casual leave—whether they feel the necessity of the same or not. Casual leave means unforeseen/ accidental leave. Sincere employees should avail of this category of leave in case of emergent/unforeseen situation only. Work of the employees should not be kept pending for availing of all categories of leave.

While the employees have to aspire for higher position, they should try to abjure availing of maximum number of days of leave so that they can work more. More the work the employees do the more they will be gravitated to the office and they will feel restless if they fail to attend office on any occasion.

Maintenance of Cordial Relations with the Superior Officers | 15

Employees must maintain sweet and cordial relations with all the officers of the Company—whether with those of the same department where the employees have been working or that of other departments. Employees have to think that the Organisation is a big family and they are the accredited members of the same. This leads to attachment to the Organisation by the employees which in effect results in accomplishment of the work entrusted to them with perfection and dedication. Close affinity between the officers and the employees is essential for an Organisation to prosper. In this connexion, it is noteworthy to mention that "Reliance, Dhirubhai Ambani would often say, has been built on the foundation of relationship and trust." The employees who are not cooperative are not suitable for the Organisation. The higher management conveys sneering attitude towards such employees, which is a retrograde step standing in the way of progress in service career of the employees.

In majority of the cases, persons are not born officers. They have to glean knowledge and experience after working for number of years before they attain competency to become officers of the company. Mingling with the officers closely and with cooperative attitude facilitating the employees to know the knotty problems being dealt with by them and the way they are solved by them help the employees develop their mental make-up. Maturity of thoughts and ideas can be implanted in the employees when they maintain cordial relations with the officers of the Organisation.

Maintenance of cordial relations with the officers helps the employees create sound position in the Organisation and in such case they go on working with free mind. Employees working with free and undisturbed mind can learn things quickly in a better way and maintenance of cordial relations with the officers plays a vital role in this respect. An employee cannot be a responsible and successful officer if he has not cultivated cooperative attitude with hearty mind from the very beginning of his working as an employee. An employee maintaining cordial relations with the officers as well as other employees of the Organisation would be in the good books of the higher management. This is very necessary for his uplift in service in future.

An employee cannot think of getting promotion in service if the management keeps distance from the employees. Cordial and cooperative attitude of employees is a very important factor, when they are desirous of working in exalted position. No ambitious employee wants to remain in the same position of employment throughout his entire service career. He must have tendency of mobility in service and with this idea in view he can definitely be crowned with success in his endeavour to become an officer of the Company. His cooperative and cordial relations with all will be conducive in this direction.

When an employee ascends to high position in service by virtue of his cooperative attitude and maintaining cordial relations, he enjoys the laurels of his exalted position, as he gets unstinted cooperation from all in the discharge of his duties. His efficiency in working is boosted up when he works in the Organisation with free mind and without cumbrousness. Efficiency in the working of an employee is the result of his maintaining sweet relations with all. It is, therefore, inferred that maintaining sweet relations has a tremendous impact on the part of an employee to create substantive position in the Organisation.

To conclude, employees aspiring for avaricious position in service must be cooperative and maintain warm relations with all and sundry. By working with all the co-employees in an atmosphere of good-will and cooperation, output of work of the employees maintaining cordial relations will be increased manifold. This will in turn create hearty rapprochement with the higher management thus widening the possibility of growth of the employees in the Organisation in the not too distant future.

To Generate Sense of Belonging to the Company | 16

A loyal and sincere employee should never think of that his primary objective is to receive salary in exchange of the work rendered by him to the Company. To be more precise, his services to the Company should not be bartered in terms of salary. His notion must be more than this. Stability of services of an employee depends largely upon the existence of the Company where he is employed. He has to grow up with the growth of the Company. His prosperity in service is interlinked with the development and prosperity of the Organisation. If the Company goes on sinking on account of financial debilitation and other factors, the stability of the services of the employees is bound to be tremulous.

Employees must not have bitter taste of the pangs of being unemployed which is the greatest foe of the educated unemployed youths of the country. When a person is employed in an Organisation by virtue of his capability and other factors, his only idea should be to converge himself with the Company thinking that it is his own Company from where his bread and butter is earned.

Employees are the pillars of the Company. Company runs by the workings of the employees. So, there should be infallible and inalienable affinity between the employees and the Company. While it is of course correct that the efficient running of the Organisation depends largely on the formulation of proper and efficient planning and stratagem of the higher management on the one side, employees' contributions in the matter of their efficient working cannot be undermined, rather it plays a vital role in stabilising the Company on rocky foundation on the other side, which is only possible when the employees think of oneness to the Organisation by the discharge of their sincere and hard working. By this, dual advantages are accrued—one the Company leaps forward to prosperity and the other the employees can conveniently think of improving their official position vis-à-vis financial status by way of increase in salary structure when the Company becomes sound financially by the sincere and hard working of the employees and developing oneness to the Company by them.

It is now undoubtedly argued that sense of belonging to the Company by the employees is extremely important which will also ensure trouble-free running of the Organisation for all the years to come and the chance of becoming the Company emaciated or sick will be done away with.

When the oneness of the employees to the Company leads to solidifying its existence, the management of such Company has also a strong affinity with the employees who in turn can think of ascending to high position in service. The crux of the question is that the employees must be sincere to their working developing sense of belonging to the Company in their own interest.

In fact, loyal employees are those who have a strong sense of belonging to the Organisation which is providing to them bread and butter for keeping their body and soul together. No employee can think of elevation of his official position if he has no sense of oneness to the Organisation where he is employed. With his sense of belonging the employee gets impetus to work for the Company in a concerted manner and his dream for elevation of position will come to a reality. Such employees are the confidants of the higher management. Employees can even reach the zenith of official position by their own endeavours, and sense of belonging to the Company is very important in this respect.

If an employee choses his occupation of life as service, he must have sense of belonging to the Company which will be an inspiration to him to work for the Company whole-heartedly. Man attains prosperity through work. It becomes an opportunity for an employee to work when he is employed in an Organisation and this opportunity to work will push him to attain prosperity with his diligent discharge of duties by developing sense of belonging to the Company.

An Employee must have Pleasing Temperament, Courtesy and Manners

17

One of the most important qualities of an employee is his pleasing temperament. An employee with pleasing temperament is a person of courtesy and manners as well as politeness which are the hall-mark of gentleness. Courtesy and good manners with pleasing temperament enhance the self-growth of an employee. It costs nothing to be courteous but pays a lot not only to the employee but to the Organisation too. An employee with pleasing temperament, courtesy and manners can imprint good impressions in the minds of the officials/executives. Gentleness and politeness of an employee increase the prestige, honour and reputation of the Organisation where he serves. An employee with ruffled and choleric disposition is destitute of courtesy and manners which are his negative point to work as an officer/Manager. An employee must have amiable and loveable habits with pleasing temperament.

When an employee is desirous of becoming an officer/ Manager of an Organisation, he must be a person of qualities. These qualities are pleasing temperament, courtesy, manners, gentleness, towering personality, politeness and courteous behaviour. These qualities inherent in employees bring them close to the senior officer/Manager. When the senior officer/ Manager is happy with the deportment of the employees, it paves the way for ascending to the high position in service by the employees, it is also pertinent to mention here that no employee can think of over night metamorphosis in the situation. He is not to be impatient to rise in service. He must feel ecstasy that a time will come when he will be crowned with success working in exalted position in the Organisation for which he should go on preparing foundation. The employee has to ensure at the same time that his pleasing temperament, courtesy, manners, gentleness, towering personality, politeness, courteous behaviour and loveable habits are not spiced with artificiality.

An employee working in the capacity of an Assistant or the like althrough his service career is devoid of enthusiasm and high aspirations. He must have the perception that man grows up from cradle and this perception is also applicable in the case of an employee working in Organisation, where he can also grow up starting from scratch. For rising high in service cool temperament of an employee is essential, because without such temperament the employee working in exalted position will get ruffled to handle voluminous work and everything will be messy and his working in high position will be a gross miscalculation.

Cool and pleasing temperament generates patience and patience is a great virtue to handle any type of clumsy work which an officer/Manager has to deal with. An employee should, therefore, be endowed with patience so that he can find plain sailing in the discharge of his duties as a senior officer/Manager after his promotion. An employee working in exalted position must have to display to the higher management that his promotion was absolutely legitimate as he has been able to prove himself quite worthy of the position by his matured ideas and all-round experience of working and this has become possible because he is a person of cool and pleasing temperament, courtesy, manners, gentleness, towering personality, politeness, courteous behaviour, loveable habits and patience.

To sum up, an employee desirous of ascending to exalted position must be obsessed with the conception always that with ruffled temperament he cannot think of working in high position rather he must have pleasing disposition which is consistent with the working in high position in service. In order, therefore, to become a successful and competent Manager, an employee must practise patience with cool temperament from the very inception of his working as Assistant and the like having pleasing disposition, courtesy and manners. These are the fruits of all seasons and for an employee they are the great virtues to facilitate rising high in service. As far as possible, an employee working in elevated position must be a thorough gentleman being enriched with the qualities as discussed in the foregoing and his working in non-managerial capacity prior to his promotion is an introductory stage to develop the qualities in question, as narrated.

Seriousness in Working and doing Work with Perfection | 18

Seriousness in working and doing work with perfection are both complementary to each other. Perfection in the working cannot be achieved unless the work is carried on with seriousness. Similarly, seriousness in working results in perfection in job. Competence of an employee is determined by his seriousness in working and the job he does with perfection. Haphazard way of working by an employee dwindles his efficiency which tells upon his future prosperity in service.

It should not be the desire of the employees that they should go on working by remaining in the same position for years together. Tendency of remaining in the same position testifies the sluggishness in the working of the employees. Such employees have no desire to grow up, as they suffer from inferiority complex. Inferiority complex of an employee is a bane. An employee should have the notion that man is the architect of his own fate and he can of course change his fate as an employee when he becomes serious in his working in consequence of which he will attain perfection in the job he does.

Job is speeded up by working with seriousness and with perfection and the employees feel relieved of their duties when the work does not get piled up. Employees also remain in free mind which leads them to work with enthusiasm. They can also work with full concentration of mind when seriousness in the working is there. All these things combinedly help the employees attain perfection in the discharge of their duties.

Seriousness in working as well as doing work with perfection speaks high of the employees. Such employees create a very good impression in the minds of the higher management that they have close affinity with the Organisation and that they work with loyalty. Higher management prefers such employees in the employ of the Organisation. In order to rise high in service the relation between the employees and the higher management should be bridged because this gives opportunity to the higher management to know about the performance of the employees before they are promoted to higher position.

It is advisable that the employees should devote to work with all seriousness and perfection so that they can step up to reach the goal of ascending to higher position in service. Working with seriousness and perfection is the barometer of the employees attaining efficiency which will go a long way to enable them to shine in employment.

19 Employees should Express their own Faults of Working Instead of Censuring their Co-employees

Employees coveting to rise high in service must be straightforward. This straightforwardness indicates his lust for progress in service. One of the traits of personality of an employee is his straight forwardness and with this personality he does not believe in hide and seek. Such employee never tries to cover up his own deficiencies of working. He believes in the maxim, "To err is human." After committing mistakes employees get opportunity to correct the same. The boldness of an employee is exhibited when he straightway expresses that it is he who has committed the wrong and not any one else. By his such expression he is endeared by his senior officer/ Manager as it exhibits his truthfulness. In the field of employment truthfulness is a great quality and virtue. Even if his senior officer/Manager reprimands the erring employee for the wrongs committed, he considers the same as a benediction, because this helps him rectify the faults and that he will be cautious in future to minimise the mistakes in his working. This will help make him perfect in his working. Perfection in the working of an employee gravitates the senior officer/ Manager which paves the way for his future prosperity in service. When an employee is in the good books of his senior officer, he earns a good name as an employee also.

An employee committing mistakes himself in his working but laying the blame on his co-employees proves that he is weak minded and is in the bereavement of stoutness of heart to express his own fault. This is nothing but a hypocrisy on the part of the employee. But, ultimately it will surface his own responsibility of doing the wrongs. Hypocrisy on the part of an employee impedes his progress in the Organisation. Such employee is not trusted upon by his co-employees and the senior officers. This hypocritical employee is kept isolated by his co-employees and he starts feeling solitary and uneasy in his working in the Organisation. Employees should bear in mind that a hypocritical employee is put to false position always and he is denigrated in the eyes of others in the Organisation.

Employees desiring to work in managerial position must have stoutness of heart and straightforwardness in their working which will command their responsibility from others. Getting respects from others is very important and essential on the part of those working in managerial position. Otherwise working in managerial capacity will be of no signification. A straightforward employee must not think of censuring his co-employees for committing wrongs in working by himself, when they are not at all at fault.

Not to Link up Quantum of Salary in Terms of Work | 20

An employee who has high aspirations in service should never link up quantum of salary in terms of work performed by him. He must have strong belief that work is primary and the question of salary an employee receives is secondary. Payment of handsome salary to an employee does not pose a constraint when he proves himself worthy of the position by virtue of his sincere and efficient services he renderes to the Organisation.

Question of pay-package should not be hotly debated in the interviews by the candidates who have innate desire to ascend to exalted position in service. If it is done, it will leave a bad impression in the minds of the interviewers because they will have the notion that the candidates are more interested in salary than work, which will not augur well for them working in the Organisation.

Many ambitious employees even apply to Organisations for employment knowing fully well that they would be getting a bit lesser salary than what they are getting from their present Organisations. Their prime objective is to grow up in the Organisations where congenial working atmosphere persists—no matter what quantum of salary would be at the initial stage of their new assignment. In some Organisations salary structure may be high but there is no prospect of employment. Such Organisations are not preferred by many of the employees aspiring for higher position.

In a reputable Organisation high quality employees are considered very much useful. By their efficient and sincere services Organisation goes on progressing in quick succession and salary of the employees is automatically enhanced on two counts—(i) looking to the sincere and efficient working of the employees and (ii) the consistent progress of Organisation. Higher management always tries to retain such employees in the Organisation with the idea that their services would be utilised in a far better way in future by placing them in high position.

Sincerity in working always pays in the long run and quantum of salary is relative. There cannot be inconsistent gap between high position in service and the quantum of salary. Otherwise, employees working in high position will lose interest in working which will be a retrograde step for the Organisation being bereaved of getting proper services of the promoted employees even if they are efficient. Salary structure of any reputable Organisation is of course standardised and the employees aspiring for high position do not feel the necessity of bargaining with the management to fix them at comfortable salary.

Employees having aspirations of rising high in service should go on working for the Organisation with sincerity of purpose and they will of course be crowned with success in their efforts to work in managerial position, and fixation of salary commensurate to their position would not pose a constraint.

An Employee must have Maturity of Thought and Conception of Working

21

Another important factor an employee needs to shoulder higher responsibilities is to develop maturity of thought and conception of working. The job a senior officer/Manager does, is mostly of intricate nature requiring exercise of brain. In order to handle such work by him maturity of thought with conception of working is of utmost necessity. Otherwise, such work cannot be accomplished.

Both the senior officer/Manager and employees work for Organisations, but there is a difference in the quality of work done by them. One of the most important points a Manager has to surmise—what would be the reaction to the action taken by him and accordingly he has to take matured decision after deliberations so that there is no adverse reaction against the action taken and the Organisation is not put to difficulty. An employee has, therefore, to get the reflection of the qualities of the senior officer/Manager by acquiring maturity of thought and conception of working by the following methods:

(a) Maturity of thought is developed by an employee when he analyses problems thread-bare and then arrives at a decision.

(b) When an employee does work closely with senior officer/Manager and gets opportunity of knowing his technique of working and the decisions he takes on number of problems after deliberations, the employee develops maturity of thought.

(c) Devoting full attention to the working and analysing the intricacies of the same develop maturity of thought.

(d) Maturity of thought is attained when an employee works with right earnest and with all seriousness.

(e) An employee should feel enthused with the novelty of work which will create conception in the same.

(f) Working repeatedly with different types of work with perfection and seriousness creates conception.

(g) Intense interest to know the unknown work develops conception of work.

(h) An employee develops conception of ideas when he gets opportunity to correct the mistakes of his working.

Developing maturity of thought and conception of working is essentially needed to work in managerial position. Employees aspiring for high position should bear in mind that success and efficiency in the discharge of duties in managerial position will be possible when they are endowed with the above traits. It should be, therefore, of paramount necessity to acquire maturity of thought and conception of ideas of working by the above methods in order to work in managerial capacity.

Not to Indulge in Loose Talks and Avoid Tendency of Criticising others

22

Employees indulging in loose talks with tendency of criticising others have the least interest to work sincerely for the Organisation. Such habits of the employees are abominable. These employees never think of upholding the prestige and honour of Organisations where they are employed. They cannot also win the hearts of the co-employees and the senior officer/Manager. Such employees feel pleasure in loose talks and criticising both the persons and the working of the persons.

Criticism has distinguishing features—one positive criticism and the other negative criticism. But, these employees are in the habit of indulging in negative criticism only both of the persons and their working. While criticising others they do not put them in high esteem. Employees having tendency of criticising others and indulging in loose talks have no self-respect also. Such employees are misfit in an Organisation. When they mostly engage themselves in loose talks and criticising others, they have no love for work and the quantum and quality of work they put in is far below the quantum of salary they receive. Management of Organisations tries to get rid of such employees as they are considered redundant in the Organisations—what to talk of their usefulness as an employee.

Employees indulging in loose talks and criticising others do not show that they hail from decent and respectable families. Good family background plays an important role in the matter of employment to work with respectability and humility. Employees with the habit of loose talks are insulated by their co-employees. Senior officer/Manager also exhibits sneering attitude towards such employees and they are not confided in discharging any work allotted to them. The future of such employees in Organisations is dull and not promising. Employees should, therefore eschew the habit of loose talks and criticising others so that they continue to work with prestige and honour like other employees and aspire for rising high in service. Criticising others is a very bad habit of employees which should be shunned in their own interest.

When an employee will work in higher position, he may of course criticise the working of the employees in positive and constructive way and not personally in order to ensure their mistake-free working. This will help the employees to be more careful and cautious in their working in future. Hence, the criticism made by the senior officer/Manager should be taken by the employees in right perspective and also they should accept the same as benediction.

Developing Competitiveness with the Co-employees doing the Same Nature of Job | 23

Employees working in unison in office must develop competitiveness doing the same nature of job. This competition in working increases the output of work as also efficiency of the employees. Increase in output of work and efficiency is essentially needed on the part of the employees which facilitates them to shoulder higher responsibilities in service. Even the newly appointed employees being inspired to notice the competitiveness in the working of their co-employees will also try to cultivate the same tendency of creating competitiveness from the very beginning of their employment and ultimately they will not lag behind in attaining efficiency of working.

Competitiveness in working of the employees has the following advantages:

(a) Employees are fully devoted to working.

(b) Pandemonium in the office is reduced to bare minimum.

(c) Work is carried on with maximum speed.

(d) Efficiency in working of the employees is increased.

(e) Employees do not create habit of leaving the work place periodically on some pretext or the other.

(f) Discipline in the office is maintained.

(g) Office runs free of affliction and with system.

(h) There is pin-drop silence in the office, as the employees are at work with competitiveness.

(i) Solemnity in the office is maintained.

Higher management has the strong inclination that work in the Organisation is carried on with utmost efficiency of the employees and that there should not be any place for the inefficient employees. Efforts of the employees by virtue of their efficient working which is the result of developing competitiveness contribute to a large extent for attaining prosperity and development of Organisations and the efficient employees are also elevated to shoulder higher responsibilities. With the expansion and development of Organisations new posts are created for the employees working in exalted positions and hence it does not pose any problem for the higher management to fit the efficient employees in such positions after the Organisation is developed and expanded.

Employees should bear in mind that through competitiveness with the co-employees, they have to augment their working efficiency if they are avaricious of mounting up the ladder of exalted positions in service. Idling away and detraction from work will make them inefficient and the prospect of continuing in their employment will be at stake, which of course no employee desires if he has to remain in the employment of an Organisation.

Self-esteem of an Employee | 24

An employee coveting to work in managerial rank must have self-esteem among other traits and qualities needed for such position, as discussed earlier. Self-esteem is defined as the way an employee knows himself thoroughly. An ambitious employee with high self-esteem accepts jobs with entire responsibility. Performing job with responsibility means that he is serious in discharging duties which augurs well for his future prosperity in the Organisation. An employee with self-esteem has the following distinguishing features:

(a) He has sense of responsibility.

(b) He is ambitious and motivated.

(c) He has confidence.

(d) He has positive attitude.

(e) He has conviction.

(f) He has sensitivity.

(g) He has modesty.

(h) He is disciplined.

(i) He has understanding.

(j) He has self-interest.

Possession of all the above traits by an employee is the result of his being a person of self-esteem. Self-esteem of an employee aspiring for high position is very important. An employee possessing self-esteem gets impetus to work with intense ardour and efficiency.

Following are the behavioural pattern of an employee who has no self-esteem:

(a) He is a man of peculiar nature.

(b) He is not willing to accept responsibility.

(c) He is in the habit of making excuses of his own faults and failures.

(d) He is self-centered.

(e) He suffers from egoism.

(f) He avoids to mingle with his co-employees intimately.

(g) His behaviour is erratic.

An employee without self-esteem is not able to live happily or work efficiently in the particular environment of an Organisation. He is not worthy to cling to managerial position without having self-esteem. In order to work in managerial capacity he must be a man of self-esteem imbibing all the qualities, as mentioned above. It is, therefore, very important that an employee should possess self-esteem. Otherwise, his chance of elevation to higher position in service is bleak. A self-esteemed employee enjoys the patronage of his senior officer/Manager and as such he feels enthused to do job entrusted to him with responsibility. Doing job with responsibility promotes employees to higher office.

Truthfulness

25

Truthfulness of an employee reflects clarity of his mind. Such an employee is a person of reliability. In service if the employee is not relied upon because of his untruthfulness, he cannot win confidence of his superior officer/Manager and without creating confidence he cannot be a successful employee. Employees ought to be truthful if they want to occupy comfortable positions which will be favourable to them to work with honour and prestige. Truthfulness in the character of an employee pays him a great deal. Such an employee is endeared and respected by all and is not kept in isolation from his co-employees. He gets all cooperations from them in the event of his finding problem with his work at any time. Interaction with the co-employees is very important. This will help him to be in oneness with the Organisation. When an employee loves work and the Organisation he serves, he remains in the good books of his superior officer/Manager.

Truthfulness of an employee creates trust. A truthful employee is an asset to an Organisation. He can be fully relied upon in matters of handling confidential matters as he proves himself to be a confidant. In order to rise high in service truthfulness of an employee is an essential ingredient. An employee must, therefore, be truthful so that he can be confided with for any confidential matters of the higher management in the capacity of his working in exalted position.

An employee is true to his words and deeds when he is truthful in his character. Such employee never believes in hide and seek policy. His dealings are always straightforward. He is open minded. Such an employee demonstrates worthy of his position and gains favour from his superiors. With his character of truthfulness he comes very close to his superior officers/ Managers and gets opportunity of learning from them the intricacies of jobs of policy matters. Such truthful employee is considered efficacious by any Organisation and much is expected of him by the management, as he is trustworthy for any job performed by him without looking to his own personal gain or favour.

An employee without the quality of truthfulness cannot work efficiently in office environments, as his co-employees will have no liking for such employee as also by his senior officer/Manager. This type of employee is always suspicious in the eyes of the higher management and as such the possibility of his elevation in service is bleak. Truthfulness is a great quality of an employee by virtue of which he is destined to be crowned with success in his service career. It is, therefore, of great importance that employees must be truthful while in employment for the sake of their uplift in service.

Keeping Sound Health and Healthy Mind

26

An employee keeping sound health and healthy mind is a person of activity which is needed most to perform work with efficiency. Ill health devours his working efficiency. Unless an employee is a person of activity he cannot do justice to the work entrusted to him. He is to be invigorated and activated with healthy mind and sound health. Smartness of an employee is very important in the discharge of his duties and this smartness could be maintained only when he is keeping healthy mind and sound health. If an employee suffers from ill health he cannot perform his duties efficiently. Such employee will be falling sick every now and then for which he will be absenting from office sporadically as a consequence of which the work of the Organisation will suffer a lot and he will not be able to do justice to the Organisation by the work entrusted to him. Efficiency in working cannot be expected of such employee and without efficiency he cannot think of rising high in service.

Efficiency of an employee could be maintained when he would keep himself busy in doing job entrusted to him, by taking care of preserving sound health and keeping healthy mind. The best course left for an employee will be that he should work with free mind. This will make him feel enthusiastic to work with strength, vigour, zeal and freshness and will animate the working spirit of the employee. Without vitalisation of working spirit the employee cannot be promising for the Organisation and if an employee is not promising for his inefficient working which is the result of his not maintaining sound health and healthy mind, his rise in service will be bleak in the Organisation.

Sometimes family troubles torment an employee and in such case his mind does not play fully to devote his attention to the working of the Organisation and the work he does is not made perfect and flawless. Apart from this, he is also not able to do work with speed, accuracy and efficiency, as he has to do the same with dejected and heaviness of mind. His efficiency dwindles in such situation, which he has to arrest in the interest of his future prosperity in service. Under the circumstances, when the employee will be intercepted from doing work with free mind because of trouble in his family, he should put a day's off from attending office. This will help resuscitate his normal state of mind to work in office next day.

In view of what has been elucidated in the foregoing, keeping healthy mind and sound health is of paramount importance on the part of an employee to work with speed, accuracy and efficiency. It is advisable that employees should be very much prudent to keep healthy mind and sound health always which is essentially needed for ascending to high position in service by the employees.

Must have Propensity to Learn Working from other Senior Employees and Officers/ Managers

27

Gleaning extensive knowledge of working is important for an employee to strengthen his position in service. A well-experienced employee with sound knowledge of working is no doubt indispensable for an Organisation. Question for promotion of an employee is considered favourably when his knowledge of working is deep-seated. Developing knowledge of working by an employee is mostly the sequence of learning from senior employees and officers/Managers. Unless an employee is guided as to how the work is to be conducted his knowledge of working cannot be sound. In order to attain maturity of working an employee has to work closely with senior employees who have more working experience. Knowledge of working of an employee is not spontaneous. An employee desiring to gather deep-seated knowledge of working for attaining prosperity in service, must have the propensity to learn from other senior employees and officers/Managers.

No employee at the initial stage of his employment is abounding with working knowledge. His working knowledge gets maturity with the lapse of years and more importantly by working closely with the senior employees with matured working knowledge. The employees who are very much voracious to work in higher position must have propensity to learn things at the quickest possible time so as to create an impression in the minds of their officers/Managers that they (employees) are intellectually sharp and developed to harness themselves with working knowledge in no time. When the officers/Managers are impressed with such employees, their future in the Organisation is no doubt bright.

A sincere and hard working employee never wastes time during the course of his working. Such employee always thinks that the work he is doing is a sport. With this sportive tendency of working he is obsessed with the belief that he is doing complete justice to the Organisation by the diligent discharge of his duties which he has learnt with the lapse of years and also from his superiors. Such employee is also at the same time very much optimistic that his knowledge of working must be rewarded by way of his promotion in high position today or tomorrow.

An employee with extensive working knowledge is evaluated very much in the field of employment. Higher management also does never want to part with such employee as his services are very much useful for the Organisation. The employee with comprehensive working knowledge never feels dejected, because the need for such an employee is with every Organisation. It is, therefore, very important on the part of an employee that he should be voracious always to learn the intricacies of working from his superiors so that the storage of knowledge gained by him will help push him up in service.

Not to Refuse doing Overtime Work on some Pretext or the other

28

Doing overtime work when situation warrants is a part of duty of an employee. No employee should shirk of his responsibility from doing overtime work on some pretext or the other. Avoiding to do overtime work by an employee is the evidence that he has no love or fascination for work for the Company, which of course does not augur well for his future prosperity in service. There is a limitation in the number of hours of overtime work in an individual month and the employees will not be required to do overtime beyond the said number of overtime hours, which will be a contravention of the principle of overtime work done.

Employees must show their loyalty to the Organisation by their sincere and hard work. In order to work in higher position they have to be saddled with work. Employees have, therefore, to be fully accustomed in doing more work in their own interest and doing overtime work is an addition to their normal work. Employees should bear in mind that doing more work keeps them healthy and happy. By keeping them fully engaged in work they will feel belonging to the Organisation and the higher management will also have leaning towards such employees. It is, however, recommended that continuous overtime work for days together should be avoided. Otherwise, it will bring fatigue which will no doubt tell upon the efficiency of employees in the long run.

The employees who are afraid of hard work cannot think of rising high in service. Close affinity between the employees and the higher management grows up when the employees show their leaning towards doing more work including overtime work. This closeness in relation with the higher management is a step in the right direction to create a sound position in service by an employee in the Organisation.

Through overtime work done by an employee periodically it shows devotion to duties by him. When an Organisation is set to march forward towards development and prosperity there increases volume of work and the employees must not shirk of from doing the same including overtime work because he has to bear in mind that with the growth of the Organisation he has also to grow up by working hard.

From what has been discussed in the foregoing it is construed that doing overtime work by an employee is a part of his duty and the employee who wants to stick to his normal duty only in the Organisation by avoiding to do overtime work will find it difficult to rise in service, as doing normal work is not always the criterion that he can shoulder load of work which is essentially needed to work in exalted position. Employees should not, therefore, feel disinclination to do overtime work in their own interest.

An Employee must not be Oily Tongue

29

An employee who is habitually a oily tongue is not sincere in his working. His intention is to gain undue favour from his superior officer/Manager through flattery. Such employee is in the bereavement of efficiency in his working. He is very sweet in his dealings, but his sweetness is spiced with artificiality. He is in the habit of blowing hot and cold in the same breath. He is not an open hearted employee and his mind is also not clean and sophisticated. Such an employee cannot be confided in on any matter. This type of employee is a misfit in Organisations.

An employee with oily tongue cannot rise high in service. His tendency is not to glean working knowledge which is essentially needed to work as an officer/Manager in the Organisation. He sounds high but with no depth. Such an employee is under the impression that by his artifice of flattery he can easily win the hearts of his superior officer/Manager. But, it is his misconception. This type of employee is never found working with seriousness. He practises the art of oiling with the purpose of cajoling his boss whenever he is in pleasant mood so as to gain something advantageous for him out of the way. Such an employee by his artifice of flattery wants to establish his position in the Organisation that he is indispensable and that he is competent enough to rise high in service.

When these are the characteristics of an employee with oily tongue, his superior officer/Manager has to be meticulous to deal with such type of employee diplomatically and cautiously. An employee with oily tongue should at the same time bear in mind that his senior officer/Manager is not a person lacking in wisdom or a person of weak mind to be beguiled easily by his artifice of flattery. If an employee is sensible and intelligent he should eschew the habit of practising flattery, as he should be in the know that this false art has no place in the Organisation and by this stratagem he cannot rise high in service.

Such an employee is not regarded with respect by others. The relation he maintains with his co-employees is counterfeit and he is kept sidetracked because his artifice of flattery is not to their liking. The future of such employee is bleak. He cannot win confidence in the minds of his senior officer/ Manager which is no doubt a minus point for him as an employee.

The crux of the question is that no employee should practise flattery and that he must not be an oily tongue, if he is sincerely desirous of rising high in service. Flattery is a mischief which has no place in any Organisation. Such an employee is not liked by anybody from the core of heart. By practising artifice of flattery an employee cannot think of ascending to high position because his knowledge cannot be attained by flattery. Such employee always believes in giving bluffs.

Sincerity in the Discharge of Duties by an Employee | 30

Sincerity has special efficacy and worth in the life of every upright and sensible human being. Progress of a man is based on sincerity. Insincere persons are always unreliable. When nobody believes an insincere person, he cannot undertake any responsible job and without accomplishing the same he cannot change his life towards prosperity. Hence, sincerity plays a very important role in the life of a human being for transformation of his destiny.

The above is also mirrored in letter and spirit in the case of an employee working in Organisation. A sincere employee can never be a failure in performing his duties assigned to him. Sincerity will pay an employee his due share of prosperity in service. Working by an employee with sincerity will help him attain dexterity and flawlessness in his job and this is the measurement of his capability as an efficient employee of an Organisation. An efficient employee is always worthy of holding high position in service. When an employee is sincere his work is never piled up and he feels easy to perform his job—whether the same is complicated or not. This helps him attain efficiency in his working in no time. Fortune is destined to smile on such sincere and efficient employee. Employees should, therefore, work with all sincerity in their own interest. Sincere employees are the assets of an Organisation and they have their growth in the same. When the employees are sincere, Organisation leaps forward to development and expansion. Hence, growth of an Organisation and growth of employees have relativity.

31 An Employee should not be Talkative

Employees who are talkative by nature get little time to attend to their work and hence their output of work is much lesser than that of their co-employees who do not believe in unproductive talks but work only. Talkative employees are irksome for others. Sincere employees are not at all friendly with the talkative employees because they know that if they commune with such employees believing in talks only they will feel disturbed in the discharge of their duties, as their value of time will be devoured in unproductive talks of the talkative employees.

Too much of unproductive talks and work cannot go hand in hand. Talkative employees have no inspiration to rise high in service. Such employees have no depth of knowledge of working. They do not also try to learn work. They cannot do work with perfection—what to talk of accelerating their output of work. There is a maxim, "Work more talk less." Since man cannot rise without work, employees should utilise more time to do maximum work without indulging in talks when they are at work. Talkative employees have no place in an Organisation because their output of work is bare minimum. Employees talking less but devoting more time to do work are destined to rise high in service. Talkative employees should, therefore, shun their bad habit of indulging in unproductive talks in their own interest.

An Employee should not Express that he Knows Everything

32

There is a proverb, "Empty vessel sounds much." If we take the case of an employee, analysis of this proverb will reveal that an employee who is practically devoid of working knowledge is in the habit of exerting himself that he knows everything mainly with the purpose of blowing his own trumpet. In doing so, he becomes nothing but a laughing stock. Such an employee wants to have his existence in an Organisation on deception. He cannot create position in the eyes of his senior officer/Manager. In fact, work performed by an employee is itself the expression of his knowledge of working and not the expression that he knows everything.

In an Organisation there are generally two categories of employees—one who know work fully but do not express that they know everything and the other who do not know much work but express that they know everything. The first category of employees creates solid position in an Organisation and it is they who rise high in service as compared to the second category of employees. It is, therefore, absolutely necessary that the employees who are not in the know of much knowledge of working should not express that they know everything, because such expression of theirs does not stand to prove that they know everything.

Apart from what has been discussed thread-bare in the foregoing analysing the various aspects which are required to be maintained and practised by the employees so as to enable them to broaden their path to ascend to high position in service from non-managerial position of employment, I have felt it necessary to throw light some of the fundamental principles through the following questions and answers which the employees ought to keep themselves abreast of the same in their own interest while working in Organisations.

An Employee should not be Envious to See that One of their Colleagues has got Promotion by Superseding him

33

It is a common feature that in commercial organisations cases for promotion of employees are considered in preference to other employees in successive stages depending upon number of factors. It cannot be expected of that all the employees in a department are fairing well together in the same proportion and hence the cases for promotion of the employees all at a time are far from expectation. The employees who have not been promoted can naturally cherish the conception that they have not yet been considered upto the mark to claim for their elevation in position. Therefore, it will be an instance for such employees that they are still lagging behind in the matter of competence and efficiency as compared to those who have been promoted. In such case, it will be a foolishness on the part of the employees not getting promotion to be despondent rather it should be an exhortation to them as to how they have to acquire competence and efficiency in the manner other employees attained the same which helped them to be promoted from their present position. If the employees not getting immediate promotion are envious with their colleague getting promotion, it will torment their minds and they will feel dejected with the consequence that it will be a retrograde step from attaining efficiency and competence in their working and that they will show dereliction in performing their duties always. The adverse effect of this will be that they will never be able to work efficiently which will stand in the way of their elevation in service in the organisation.

Under the circumstances, the only course left for the employees is to emulate the working efficiency of their colleague getting promotion in service. The employees not getting promotion must take things easy and normal and cooperate with the promoted employees in all respects and try to work more efficiently to gain favour from the Management so that they can also get promotion like them in the not too distant future. Dissatisfying the Management by not working efficiently no employee can think of elevation in his position and to become envious with the promoted employees will be a step in the wrong direction on his part. It is always desirable that all employees not getting promotion must be inspired and rejuvenated to follow the foot-print of their promoted employee — no matter he was their colleague before his promotion.

Employees with sky-rocketing ambition in life must go on working sincerely and their endeavour to work with efficiency must be rewarded when they will be elevated to high position in service at the instance of their colleague working in exalted position. They should bear in mind that sincerity, honesty and efficiency in their working will never go unheeded, which may be a question of time only.

Submissiveness in the Attitude of an Employee

34

An employee must be submissive in his attitude while working in any Organisation. Employees with submissiveness are endeared by their co-employees as also the officers. For an employee submissiveness is a virtue and a great qualification.

Arrogant employees cannot think of elevation in position because they are always side-tracked both by the officers and the co-employees. These employees cannot glean experience of working because they cannot expect of any cooperation from anyone and hence knowledge of their working remains shallow and partial. Arrogant employees are always indisciplined and as such they spoil the entire discipline of the Organisation. Such employees do not allow other employees to work with devotion. The Management dislikes these arrogant employees and tries to get rid of them from the Organisation. Hence, employees with arrogant attitude have no place in any Organisation—what to think of their elevation in service.

Employees with submissiveness in attitude are an asset for any Organisation. They are problem-free for the co-employees and also the officers. Such employees are always extended with helping hand from all and sundry. Employees with submissiveness are not ill-tempered at any time. This helps them immensely to glean extensive knowledge of working, as they get all assistance and cooperation from all. Acquiring sound knowledge of working is a positive step for them to ascend to the ladder of high position in service. Cool disposition is expected of an employee when he is submissive. This cool disposition is extremely necessary when an employee being placed in high position has to deal with multifarious problems without becoming ruffled in temperament. An officer with choleric disposition is a failure in his service to the Organisation. He cannot shoulder higher responsibilities as the higher Management never considers placing such employee in high position for the sake of efficient working of the Organisation.

From what has been elucidated in the foregoing, there are two types of employees—one with arrogant attitude and the other with submissiveness in temperament. While an arrogant employee has no place in any Organisation denying all scope for him to attain high position in service, a submissive employee has always the support of all and gets all assistance for gleaning comprehensive knowledge of working which clears his ways to the attainment of exalted position in service. It is, therefore, suggested that the employees who have to earn their livelihood from service to the Organisations must be submissive in attitude and temperament. Such employees are also complacent of their permanency in the job as the higher Management is not willing to part with such employees.

35

An Employee must not Think that his Ambition has been Fulfilled by Getting Employment

Without ambition life is sterile and meaningless. Ambition is the mother of success. A man becomes great when he is devoted to work with the object of implementing his ambition. There are two types of employees—one who is desperately in search of employment and when he gets job he is fully satisfied that his ambition has been crowned with success and the other whose absolute inclination is to devote to work in such a way that he ascends to the echelon of high profile job. Ambition of such employee is sky-rocketting which he implements by virtue of his sincere and hard working. He is always voracious to learn the complexities of work and contemplates ways and means to arrive at a honourable and upright solution of such complex job so that his mind is made fertile to prove his capability to shoulder any high profile job with ease and comfort.

The employees who think that his ambition has been fulfilled by getting employment are derelict of inspiration. Such employees continue to remain in the same position of employment throughout their entire service career. Needless to mention—man is the architect of his own fate. By virtue of his endeavour and perseverance man can forsake profligacy and can rise to lofty position in life. This is also evidently applicable in the case of the employees who can also rise from humble position if he has the inclination to prosper in life by his devotion to job.

Comfortable education of an employee plays a significant role to help him attain qualitative position in service because education fertiles his brain which enables him to thrash out problems which he may face during the course of his employment. Hence, the employees who are not rich in education should prosecute studies in night shift colleges with due knowledge to the concerned management official.

No employee should feel despondent that he has no future in the Organisation. His future is in his own hands in the sense that the responsibility lies with him to come in the limelight of the higher management by proving himself that he is hard working, efficient and that he is well equipped with the working of which he is entrusted with. He must not think that his ambition has been carried into effect after he has got employment. After his employment he has to go a long way to implement his ambition to ascend to high ranking job for which he has to devote himself fully to working of the organisation. He must bear in mind the saying: "Industry is the mother of success". His success in service career will never go unheeded when he has high ambition to fulfill by his hard and sincere working by abjuring the idea that after he has got employment his ambition has been fulfilled.

Employees Aspiring for High Position have to Learn How to Make Independent Correspondence

36

One of the important and essential prerequisites on the part of the Officers/Managers is that they have to be fully conversant with the art of making independent correspondence. Otherwise, their working in the Organisation will not be complete and full-fledged. It is not the fact that these Officers/Managers have learnt independent correspondence at a later stage when they started working in exalted position.

Standard and matured correspondence augments the reputation and prestige of an Organisation. There is no denying the fact that correspondence is the mouth-piece of any Organisation. It is a powerful instrument to maintain link and correlation with other Organisations which helps thriving business activities. Officers/Managers who are not adept in making matured and standard correspondence are not successful in their profession. Hence, knowledge of correspondence is very important for working in exalted position especially in commercial Organisations.

There are ways as to how to glean knowledge of making correspondence. The employees who have the innate inclination to ascend to high position in service must bear in mind that without the knowledge of making correspondence it will be a problem for them to clear their ways to ascend to high position in service. They should, therefore, devote much attention to the learning of making independent correspondence during the course of their working in non-Managerial capacity.

For attaining the knowledge of correspondence the following methods are to be adopted:

(a) It is very necessary that matters are expressed in letters in simple English and in lucid form.

(b) Commercial correspondence should be concise. Otherwise, the readers of the same will feel irksome to go through lengthy correspondence. The letters should also be to the point.

(c) For drafting out letters the employees must have comfortable knowledge of English. If any of the employees is deficient in English, he should develop its knowledge for which he should read English newspaper regularly and also should have a book like "How to Learn Flawless English" available in the market which will help the employees enrich their knowledge of English.

(d) Employees should develop the habit of drafting out simple letters at the initial stage in pursuance with the points and outlines mentioned by their departmental heads on which the letters are to be drafted out.

(e) With due permission of the departmental heads the employees should go through the correspondence files which will be a guidance to them as to how the letters are made out.

(f) In order to develop knowledge of correspondence it is suggested that the employees may get themselves admitted in some reputable college of correspondence.

It is also very important that the employees who have not attained maturity of thought and conception of working will not feel it easy to draft out letters. In order to attain the same the employees have to follow the under-noted methods:

(i) An employee can develop maturity of thought when he analyses problems thread-bare. His maturity of thought will also be developed when he closely works with his departmental head and understands how the decisions are taken by him.

(ii) Devoting full attention to the working and analysing the intricacies of the same develop maturity of thought.

(iii) Intense interest to know the unknown work develops conception of work.

(iv) An employee develops conception of ideas when he gets opportunity to correct the mistakes of his working.

No employees should expect that his knowledge of correspondence will have maturity overnight. He will go on developing the same consistently when the above instructions are followed by him with right earnest.

Employees must be Ambitious and Enthusiastic | 37

Ambitious employees are the architects of shaping their own future career. There is a saying, "As you sow so you reap". And accordingly, the employees will reap the harvest as they sow. Barring aside a few, employees are not born officers. Instances are plenty that many non-managerial employees have become Officers/Managers. This has become possible when the employees have ambition to grow up. Ambition is destined to mould future career of employees. Man develops from cradle and so is the case with the employees. When an employee works in an Organisation he gets enough scope to embellish his working environments and when he harnesses himself with different types of working he can reasonably expect to be placed in high position in service and in such case his ambition plays a dominant role. It is an axiomatic fact that high ambition is the mother of success. Therefore, when an employee works in right direction with ambition to rise high in service, he is sure to achieve his goal. Employees without ambition are rudderless. Such employees in spite of having plenty of resources in themselves cannot put into active service which becomes a retrograde step to achieve qualitative position in service. Ambition enlivens the employees to devote themselves fully to the work of which they are entrusted with. They should bear in mind that ambition and prosperity are inter-linked and so without ambition there cannot be attainment of prosperity. Therefore, employees must have definite ambition to attain prosperity in service.

Side by side with ambition employees should also be enthusiastic. An employee with dereliction of enthusiasm cannot be ambitious. An employee who is enthusiastic is always voracious to do effective job in the office and by doing effective job he becomes efficient and the efficiency in his working leads him to be ambitious. An employee who is not efficient cannot be ambitious because ambition stands on sound footing which is based on deep working knowledge of an employee. Hence, enthusiasm and ambition are complementary to each other and these two traits help an employee to rise high in service. An enthusiastic employee never idles away in the office excepting in the case when he feels weary. It has been seen that the employees who have been promoted to exalted position were enthusiastic and ambitious. These two traits helped them to be efficient when they were working in non-managerial capacity before their elevation in position.

No employee should feel that his ambition has been fulfilled after his getting employment else he will continue to remain in the same position throughout his entire service career. He must think of his mobility by his ambition and enthusiasm. Tendency to grow up must be there in every employee so that he can enjoy the fruits of his coveted position.

Employees have to Build Self-Confidence | 38

Self-confidence means full belief and trust in oneself. It also means self-respect and self-esteem. A positive attitude is a pre-requisite for self-confidence. An employee having self-confidence ascribes himself of a strong personality. Self-confidence is the most excellent guiding force of a person's onward march towards attaining successful career. Employees possessing self-confidence can speak assertively and do anything with self-determination. It also generates a feeling in the minds of the employees that they can do everything possible. A person of self-confidence is a person of firm will. Goethe has said, "He who is of firm will moulds the world to himself". Self-confidence helps overcome doubts, does away with apprehension and creates healthy attitude towards everything in life. Self-confidence is, therefore, very important for an employee to rise high in service.

Now, the question arises as to how to develop self-confidence. While self-confidence cannot be developed overnight, employees can attain it by following the under-noted guidance:

(a) The employees who are devoid of self-confidence are obsessed with trepidation and fear. Employees lacks in reasoning power if they are in the deprivation of self-confidence. In such circumstances, they need spirit to overcome fear and trepidation. Hence, it is advisable to dispel fear from the personality of the employees.

(b) Self-confidence and will power are complementary to each other. Success of an employee comes only through will power. Failure is there when will power of an employee is not strong. Therefore, employees have to cultivate the habit of strong will power.

(c) Success or failure is caused more by mental attitude than by mental capacities. Employees, therefore, have to develop mental attitude in such a manner that they can dispel fear and do any work without any problem.

(d) Employees should analyse what are their shortcomings which can be overcome by them by courage and confidence. Also if any employee has inferiority complex he should try to remove it. This can be done by socialising with people.

(e) In order to develop self-confidence an employee must have positive attitude with conviction. He must feel sure of anything and that he should be always prepared to take risk as he has full confidence in himself.

Self-confidence is a very important and essential elemental part of an employee. Employees will have to work with self-confidence which will help them ascend to high position in service. Self-confidence broadens periphery of working for a prospective employee. Every employee should, therefore, develop self-confidence by the practice of the above guidelines and in doing so he is detained to thrive in his service career.

39 Mental Alertness and Consistency

Mental alertness of an employee is an important attribute for his distinctive personality. For widening the scope of rising in service mental alertness of an employee is a very important factor. An employee with mental alertness has the following characteristics:

(a) Relaxed attitude and presence of mind,

(b) Quickness in arriving at conclusions and taking correct decisions,

(c) Quickness in grasping other's viewpoint,

(d) Mental nimbleness and swiftness of observation,

(e) Quickness of thinking,

(f) Quick understanding of problems.

An employee aspiring for ascending to the position of an Officer/Manager must be in the know that alertness is an important quality in an officer that enables him to control the employees and the Organisation and when he will be in such position he will also be required to control the same by his alertness of mind in similar manner. An employee must be mentally vigilant and possess a quick and sharp observation power. He should be free from all confusions.

In order to develop mental alertness an employee has to follow the under-noted guidelines:

(a) An employee has to give full concentration and attention to his working,

(b) An employee needs acute observation powers for developing presence of mind,

(c) An employee has to pay too much of attention to what his departmental Manager explains. This will develop his grasping power.

As far as consistency is concerned, the employee should be consistent throughout in his opinion *i.e.*, he should not swing while expressing his opinion. He will remain firm in his temper, actions and thoughts. He should not change his viewpoints with the purpose of pleasing his superior officers. If done so, it will prove that he is an employee of vacillation, which will not speak high of him for considering his case by the Management for placing him in high position in service. Change of opinion and viewpoints will depict his lack of maturity and consistency. Maintaining consistency by an employee shows his strong character.

From the above elucidations it comes out crystal clear that mental alertness and consistency are two important attributes for a well-balanced and impressive personality of an employee. Possession of these two attributes combinedly will pave the way for ascending to the exalted position by an employee. Accordingly, there should be mental alertness of an employee as also he should be consistent in his temper, action and opinion and thinking.

Other Traits of an Employee Needed for Rising High in Service

40

(a) Employees must have patience

Methodical way of working without excitement conduces an employee to become efficient. An employee must not be ruffled in temperament to see the spate of work. Otherwise, he cannot be expected to shoulder higher responsibilities in his working in the capacity of a Manager. Employees have to work with patience which is a great virtue. Attainment of perfection in the working of an employee is possible when he works with calm and patience. This perfection of working attained by an employee is indispensable for him to pave the way for rising high in service. An employee who is impatient is a failure in the discharge of his services to the Organisation. Such an employee is a misfit for any business enterprise. A patient employee is an asset to the employer because such an employee can fulfil the expectations of the higher Management. Enlightened Management always wants to utilise the services of such employees in higher position who have attained efficiency in their working by their perseverance and patience.

(b) Way of walking of an employee

It is always desirable that the employees have to cultivate a "dashing forward" way of walking. The employees who are smart in walking have ambition to rise high in service by conquering all impediments which hinder progress. Character of an employee can be analysed by his way of walking. A confident employee walks with smartness. Also by the way he walks his personality is exhibited. Confident and ambitious employees take firm and decisive steps while walking. When smartness of walking is one of the pre-requisites of rising high in service, employees must have to cultivate a "dashing forward" way of walking. This shows his personality also. An employee with personality has edge over others to be in the lime-light of the higher Management.

(c) Way of Expression of an Employee

Clarity in the expression is very important an employee should possess. The tone of the voice should be clear. Employees should keep a pleasant expression while speaking and should not rush through sentences at high speed so that the listeners can follow with ease what they utter. The expression of a Manager must be clear and free from ambiguity so that the instructions he gives are not misunderstood by his subordinates and no problem is faced by them while executing his instructions/orders. Therefore, the employees aspiring for working in managerial position have to improve their way of speaking. It is not necessary that while speaking with clarity the employees have to speak with loud voice.

(d) Appearance of an Employee

An employee can be presentable in his appearance even if he is not good looking. It is a fact that all the educated Indians of all the provinces are not good looking. Still then many of them are working in exalted position in service. Appearance of an employee plays a very important role for rising high in service. Appearance includes overall look which depends mainly upon attire, hairstyle and facial expressions. It makes a real impact on others. Following are the essences to be presentable in the appearance of an employee:

(i) *Dress*: Dress is always important. Proper dress an employee wears enhances his appearance. The dress should not be out-dated. Wearing of dress made of jeans has to be avoided. Clean and well creased attire is far more important. Pair of socks should be matching to the colours of the full pant an employee wears, wearing costumes with dazzling colour should be avoided, which will not speak of good taste of the employee.

(ii) *Hairstyle and shoes.* Hair should be neatly combed. Male employees without beard should have regular shaving. This will project healthy look. Employees should also pay equal attention to their shoes which should look clean and well-polished.

(iii) *Facial expression.* It is said that face is the reflection of one's mind. An employee with pleasant smile creates a favourable impression on others. Others do not have good impression on the employees who have a long and serious face.

Overall Instructions to the Employees

Employees will find that as many as 40 points have been discussed in this book giving specific chapter-wise instructions to them to follow so that they can rise to the lofty position in service. Such instructions to the employees are very important which can make them perfect in their working by which they can be elevated to higher position. While it will not take very long time to get themselves acquainted fully with all the instructions contained in this book, every employee must go through this book with the purpose of gleaning all-round experience as the instructions are extremely valuable for them.

Exercise

QUESTIONS AND ANSWERS

Q. 1. Is bonus an employee's right? When an Organisation is losing, is it obligatory on the part of the owner to pay bonus? What is the difference between statutory bonus and bonus under a private agreement?

Ans. Under Section 1 of the Payment of Bonus Act, 1965, employees of every factory/office employing 20 or more persons on any day in an accounting year, have statutory right to receive bonus, provided they worked for at least 30 working days in an accounting year. Section 36 of the Act empowers the Government to exempt an establishment from the provisions of the Act having regard to certain factors, *e.g.*, financial position thereof. An employee has a right to receive bonus irrespective of the fact whether the employer is making profit or not particularly when the payment of bonus was initiated earlier in the Organisation.

Statutory payment of bonus is made as per the Payment of Bonus Act, 1965. On the other hand, the employer and the employees may arrive at an agreement or settlement regarding payment of bonus payable to the employees in line with the provisions of the 1965 Act to determine the minimum quantum of bonus payable.

Q. 2. If a Company declares closure of its undertaking, what is the consequence left for the employees? What are the remedies open to the employees?

Ans. Section 2(cc) of the Industrial Disputes Act, 1947, defines "closure" as closing down of a place of employment or part thereof. The consequence for the employees is that their services are terminated. If it is a case of genuine closure, the employees are only entitled to notice and compensation as per Section 25-FFF of the 1947 Act. If the undertaking is closed down under unavoidable circumstances, the compensation shall not exceed an employee's three months average pay. Unavoidable circumstances do not include factors like financial difficulties/losses of the employer.

If the closure is a stratagem for a lockout under Section 2(1) of the Industrial Disputes Act, 1947 which means temporary suspension of work to counteract workmen's collective bargaining, the validity of the closure may be challenged before the Industrial Tribunal by the workmen concerned.

Q. 3. At the time of leaving a Company an employee has not received his final settlement and in the meantime the Company has also changed its name. Under the circumstances, what is the way out to get his due payment from the Company?

Ans. If an employee had left the Company without transgressing the terms of employment and also he is legally entitled to get all his dues from the Company, for which they (Company) are dilly-dallying to clear his dues, the employee can always put his claim of getting the dues payable to him by the previous Company by filing a civil suit. If the Organisation is a government one, he can proceed under Article 226 of the Constitution of India against the employer. In the matter of getting payment of his dues, it does not matter that the Company has changed its name subsequently.

Q. 4. Is it justified that a Company can issue termination letter to its employees giving three/one months' notice, as the case may be, as stipulated in the appointment letters, without assigning any reason thereof? In such case, can the employee fight it out?

Ans. As per Article 226 of the Constitution, an employee can of course challenge the arbitrary decision of the employer in terminating his services without assigning any reason. This will be in the case of the employee working in public sector company, as such Company cannot deal with its employees in arbitrary manner, although in the appointment letter it may be written clearly in one of the clauses that the services of the employee can be terminated after confirmation of his services by giving three/one months' notice or pay in lieu thereof without assigning any reason thereof.

In the case of working in a private limited Company/ unless the employees are protected under the Industrial Disputes Act, it may not be possible to win success in filing case against the employer in the above situation. The basic reason is that the employee has accepted the terms of employment and the service rules of the Company by signing the duplicate copy of the appointment letter. The only consolation is that such a clause in the appointment letter is contrary to public policy and so it may go in favour of the employees other than working in managerial capacity.

Q. 5. Will it be in order to put an employee on probation for a period of 12 months?

Ans. An employee who is put on probation on appointment is against permanent vacancy. On successful completion of probationary period, the employee is confirmed in his services. The purpose of putting the employee on probation is to gauge his working before confirmation. As per labour law, an employee either he is appointed on training or on probation is eligible to claim permanency in his job after completion of 240 days of working and in this case he does not need to complete 12 months of training/probation. Therefore, it will be in the fitness of things if the training/probationary period is fixed initially for six months with provision for extension of the period by another three months.

In many Organisations trainees are appointed (not as per the Apprentices Act, 1961) when they have no working experience and they are paid remuneration on lump-sum basis in the form of allowance, which is fixed on higher side as salary on confirmation in line with the salary of other employees of similar rank.

As a good employer it is always better to stick to the labour laws in toto in all respects and any deviation from the same may lead to problems and complications.

Q. 6. Can the services of a confirmed employee be terminated if he takes unauthorised leave after expiry of sanctioned leave?

Ans. Absence from duty unauthorisedly by a confirmed employee after expiry of his sanctioned leave is no doubt a misconduct on his part, but on this ground his services cannot be terminated, as per the ruling given by the Allahabad High Court. The erring employee cannot be denied the right to explanation or an opportunity of hearing in the event of his being removed from services for taking unauthorised leave. Justice S.N. Srivastava of Allahabad High Court gave the ruling on a writ petition filed by Messrs DCM Limited, Ghaziabad. It is however, pertinent to mention here that the unauthorised leave should be within the reasonable number of days.

Q. 7. Can an employee go on remaining on unauthorised leave for months together on some pretext or the other after expiry of his sanctioned leave?

Ans. In public service leave cannot be claimed as a matter of right. Extending leave unauthorisedly after expiry of sanctioned leave is no doubt a misconduct on the part of an employee. Non-reporting to duties for months together after expiry of sanctioned leave may attract serious consequences if the employer is of the opinion that such unauthorised absence amounted to gross misconduct on the part of the employee. If the employee does not report for duties within specified time even after receiving letter from the employer, the name of such employee could be removed from the role of the Company.

Alternatively, if the employee goes on extending leave, it is the discretion of the employer whether to condone such long absence or not. If, however, the employer is fully satisfied with the genuine reasoning and/or tragic circumstances adduced by the employee for his long absence from duty, drastic action may not be taken by the employer for such long absence of the employee on compassionate ground/special circumstances and such extended leave of the employee may be treated as extraordinary leave without pay, if no earned leave is due to the credit of the employee for adjustment from the same.

The above is applicable in case of a confirmed employee.

Q. 8. Is a probationary employee entitled to avail of leave during the period of his probation?

Ans. Appointment of a probationary employee is against permanent vacancy. On confirmation of his services he is taken on permanent cadre. During the period of his probationary service he is not entitled to avail of any category of leave. If he remains absent from duty on any day before he is confirmed in his services, he will be on loss of pay. Such employee will, however, continue to accrue earned/privilege leave from the date of his joining. He will be entitled to avail of this category of leave only after one year of confirmation of his services. As regards casual leave, he will not accrue the same during the period of his probationary service. He will be entitled to avail of this category of leave after confirmation of his services on pro-rata basis. It is pertinent to mention here that different categories of leave allowed by Organisations are not as per statute.

Q. 9. Is it in order to terminate an employee without assigning any reason during the period of probation?

Ans. The fact is that a probationer cannot claim to be a permanent employee till such time he is confirmed in his services, although a probationer is appointed against a permanent vacancy. If, however, the management has to dispense with the services of a probationary employee, it will be in the fitness of things and an act of genuine labour practice to issue him a letter asking him to be more particular in the discharge of his duties during the extended period of his probationary service by another three months or so, as stipulated in the letter of appointment. This means that he is to be given chance to improve upon his performance during probation and that the union leaders will also be satisfied that by such letter the management has given opportunity to the incumbent to improve upon his working before he is confirmed. Even if his performance is not found satisfactory during the extended period of probation, his services may be terminated. In this connexion, it is pertinent to mention here that in the letter asking the probationary employee to improve upon his performance, the Management has to mention specifically the shortcomings in the discharge of his duties, without which the letter in question will not hold good.

Q. 10. If a probationary employee is not issued letter confirming his services after completion of his probationary period/s is it correct to assume that such employee is still on probation?

Ans. When the concerned employee has successfully completed his probationary period/s, he is automatically confirmed in his services from the next date of expiry of probationary period/s, even if letter confirming his services has not been issued by the Management. However, in order to make the service records file of the employee complete and up-to-date, it is necessary that such letter has to be issued at a later date, if it was not issued immediately, on completion of probationary period/s.

Q. 11. Supposing, an employee has already completed 6/9 months probationary period/s as per the terms of appointment letter but no letter of confirmation was issued to him by the appointing authority after completion of probationary period/s. In such circumstances, can the employee tender resignation without giving one/three months notice, as the case may be, which a confirmed employee is required to do after confirmation of his services?

Ans. It is an admitted fact that if an employee could complete the probationary period/s as per the terms of appointment letter, he is automatically confirmed in the post, although no letter of confirmation was issued to him by the appointing authority. But in absence of any letter of confirmation, an employee could surely tender resignation without giving any notice period for taking up employment elsewhere, for the very specific reason that non-issuance of letter of confirmation after successful completion of probationary period by the employee is the fault on the part of the appointing authority and in such case the Management has to accept the resignation without claiming any notice pay, although he is a confirmed employee without letter of confirmation. In fact, the employee has to get documentary evidence of his confirmation by way of a letter.

Q. 12. Can an employee submit resignation during the currency of availing of leave?

Ans. It is not proper on the part of an employee to submit resignation during the period of availing of leave. If any employee has in mind to submit resignation he has to report back on duty first after expiry of leave or after cutting short of his sanctioned leave and then submit resignation. Management is not, therefore, bound to accept such resignation of an employee, if it is submitted during the currency of availing of leave. In such case, the employee cannot go to the court of law for non-acceptance of resignation by the management and non-settlement of his dues in the event of his resignation submitted during the period of his availing of leave.

Q. 13. If an employee submits resignation either with immediate effect or with effect from a subsequent date, which has been accepted by the Management and if the employee withdraws it by a latter subsequently, should the management consider his letter of withdrawal of resignation?

Ans. After submitting letter of resignation by an employee, if it is accepted by the management, the request of the employee by a letter for withdrawal of his resignation may not be acceded to, because after accepting the resignation it is the discretion of the Management whether to give due consideration of the letter of withdrawal of resignation of the employee or not. On the other hand, if the management has not accepted the resignation immediately and the employee has requested the management by a letter desiring to withdraw his resignation, the management will not find any ground to accept his resignation and in this case the original letter of resignation of the employee will be nullified.

Q. 14. Can employee refuse to carry out his transfer orders?

Ans. If the service regulation stipulates that the job is transferable, the employee has to carry out the transfer orders, provided the transfer of the employee has been necessitated arising out of exigency of circumstances. If, however, the transfer of the employee is with malafide intention of the management or when the transfer is effected in contravention of service regulation, the employee concerned can go to the court of law for redressal, but in this case the employee will start realising uncomfortable situation to work with the Organisation, as the Management will not take in good taste of such behaviour of the employee. It is also the experience that the court does not interfere generally in the matter of transfer of employees as the management is always ready to place convincing reason for transfer of the employees.

Q. 15. If an employee submits resignation by serving one month's/three months' notice, as the case may be, in terms of appointment letter and the employer is refusing to release him, can he join his new assignment without acceptance of resignation letter?

Ans. Without acceptance of resignation letter which is submitted in terms of agreement/appointment letter, the employee can of course take up his new assignment and the employer cannot legally prevent the employee from taking up the new job. In such case, the management at least can withhold payment of dues of the employee till such time he hands over the charges. Release letter is also not mandatory unless otherwise it is demanded by the new employer. If, however, the new employer insists upon it which is most likely, the employee leaving the Organisation can impress upon the erstwhile employer to issue the same (release order) and they have to issue it especially when the employee has submitted resignation strictly in terms of agreement/ appointment letter.

Q. 16. When an employee is reverted as punishment for the offence committed by him, is it worthwhile that his salary has to be reduced for the lower position?

Ans. It will not be in order to reduce salary on account of demotion of the employee for the reason that the financial benefits which he was getting during the time of his erstwhile position are not curtailed. But while granting him annual increment, after allowing fitment, if it is felt necessary, the rate of increment should be in line with the graded increment for the position he holds after demotion. If, however, his salary has reached the last stage of the gradation of the demoted position, he should not be allowed any increment *i.e.*, there will be sealing in his salary till such time he will remain in the demoted position.

Q. 17. After an employee quits employment of an Organisation, can the erstwhile employer institute disciplinary proceedings against, that employee on corruption charge or the like?

Ans. When an employee quits employment of an Organisation there is no longer the existence of employee-employer relation and hence the employer does not have any *locus standi* to institute disciplinary proceedings against the ex-employee, as the charges, if there were any against the said employee, were not detected by the employer before he was released from employment. If the disciplinary action is still instituted after release of the employee, he can always approach the court for quashing the same. It may, however, be noted that the erstwhile employer at best can institute some other independent legal action against the ex-employee, even if he is not the employee of the Organisation?

Q. 18. Under what circumstances an employee could be placed under suspension while issuing him a letter of charge-sheet?

Ans. In point of fact, service rules of an Organisation provide for suspension of employees under the following circumstances:

(a) When an employee commits grievous offence for which his attendance to duties is pernicious pending finalisation of the disciplinary proceedings, he is placed under suspension while issuing him letter of charge-sheet.

(b) Suspension orders can also be issued as a penalty for offence of serious nature committed by an employee.

The suspended employee is entitled to subsistence allowance equivalent to one-third of his salary so long as he remains under suspension. Such employee is also asked to report in person to the concerned official daily during the period of suspension.

Q. 19. While accepting the letter of an employee for voluntary retirement by the Management, stating that the release order would follow shortly, can the employee withdraw the said letter before he is finally released under V.R.S.?

Ans. The Supreme Court of India clarified that the relationship between the employer and the employee is not terminated by the mere acceptance of the application for voluntary retirement till such time the employee is actually released from service against release order subsequently issued by the Management after the acceptance of the letter of the employee. Under the circumstances, the employee could withdraw his application although the same (application) was accepted by the Management but not released from service under V.R.S. by the release order.

Q. 20. Can the employer of an Organisation deny payment of gratuity to an employee dismissed from service on ground of moral turpitude and/or fraud/financial irregularities?

Ans. It is the usual norm that gratuity payment is made to an employee at the time of leaving the employment either on retirement or resigning, after completion of five years of service, in acknowledgement of the unblemished services rendered by him to the Organisation. Therefore, if an employee is dismissed from the services of a Company on ground of moral turpitude and/or fraud/financial irregularities, he is debarred from the entitlement of payment of gratuity, because his services under such circumstances are not free from blemish.

Q. 21. Should there be any privacy for an employee in the workplace?

Ans. If an employee during the course of his working in the workplace wants to maintain his privacy in the case of mails, e-mails, phone calls, etc., which include his private communications and in such case if the employer wants to monitor the same, the employee is debarred from taking recourse to law to protect himself from such privacy, because there is indeed no right to privacy in the workplace. In fact, there is no statute in India that treats 'privacy' as a protectable right for an employee.

Q. 22. What is the difference between salary/wages and remuneration/emoluments?

Ans. Salary/wages is that amount only which is paid to an employee for the services rendered by him in a month. This amount excludes any other financial benefits. On the other hand, remuneration/emolument is that amount which includes overall financial benefits an employee gets in an Organisation for the services rendered *inter alia* salary/wages. Therefore, the amount of remuneration/emolument is much more than the amount of salary/wages.

Q. 23. What is the difference between the words, 'dismissal' and 'termination' of services of an employee?

Ans. In Organisations there is the use of two words—one is 'dismissal' and the other is 'termination'. As far as meaning of these two words is concerned, they are synonymous. These two words are used in the case of dispensation of the services of employees. The word, 'dismissal' is used when the services of an employee are done away with on ground of moral turpitude and/or fraud/financial irregularities, rowdy behaviour or any other grievous offences committed, as stipulated in the Standing Orders of the Organisation.

As far as the word, 'termination' is concerned, this word is not applied for dispensation of services of employees on ground of grievous misconduct committed. When the services of employees are done away with as per terms of appointment letter/agreement entered into with the Organisation *i.e.*, without committing any offence, the word, 'termination' is used.

Q. 24. Is it obligatory on the part of an employee to obtain permission from the appropriate authorities of an Organisation for prosecuting higher studies?

Ans. If there is a condition in the service rules of an Organisation that the employee has to obtain permission from the appropriate authorities for prosecuting higher studies he has to abide by the same so as to enable him to be eligible for one step increment in addition to his usual increment or promotion, as the case may be, when he will be successful in passing the examination.

In defiance of this service condition if the employee does prosecute higher studies, which in other ways means without the knowledge of the higher management, such employee is obviously debarred from getting one step higher increment or promotion and he cannot legally claim the same.

However, in absence of service rules to this effect in any Organisation, it is not of course obligatory on the part of an employee to obtain permission for prosecuting higher studies during the course of his employment; but it is desirable to seek permission from the management to improve his academic qualification which will pave the way in strengthening his case for higher increments or promotion in the Organisation in future.

Q. 25. What are the factors on which an employee can build cordial relations with his superior officer?

Ans. Maintenance of cordial relations by the employees with their superior officers is an absolute necessity. This will gravitate the employees to work with zeal and enthusiasm. This will also create sense of belonging to the Organisation by the employees. Following are the factors on which the employees can develop cordial relations with their superior officers:

(a) The first and foremost task of an employee will be to know the style of working of his superior officer so as to enable him to work in the same line of his working. This will not create any disagreement in opinion between the employee and the superior officer. If, however, the employee disagrees with him on any point, he should express his disagreement with humility.

(b) An employee should not be a 'Yes' man. But, at the same time, he should not become overbearing. Moreover, he should not of course oblige, but can always speak obligingly and should show respect to the chair.

(c) While dealing with the superior officer, he should be alert and diligent.

(d) He should remain agreeable most of the time and honest. This will ensure confidence in the integrity of the employee.

(e) He should be always at the beck and call of his superior officer and be prompt in his working, as advised.

Q. 26. During the course of employment one of the employees' colleagues has got promotion. In such situation, will the employees envy him and what will be the dealings with him?

Ans. It will be an utter foolishness on the part of employees to envy their colleague on his promotion. They should bear in mind that it is not feasible that a number of employees could get promotions all at a time or at immediate successive stages. An employee who is found the fittest has to get promotion in preference to others. To be envious of the promotion of their co-employee is indicative of the parochialism of the employees not getting promotion. Mind of such employees will be tormented and their working will be at a low ebb which will be a retrograde step to boost up their efficiency in working. They should maintain all cooperation with their promoted colleague in all respects, which will speak highness of their minds. Their dealings with him should also continue to be affable, which will help maintain team spirit. At the instance of such promotion of their colleague the best course for the employees will be to go on working with utmost zeal and efficiency so that the next turn of promotion is stored for them in the not too distance future.

Q. 27. What is the difference between a Public Limited Company and a Private Limited Company?

Ans. A Public Limited Company is formed by a minimum of 7 (seven) subscribers and there is no maximum limit to the number of shareholders. A foreign national or a non-resident Indian can also be a shareholder subject to the approval of the Reserve Bank of India. Having wide membership by a Public Limited Company, a number of regulatory provisions are made under the Company law to exercise control over the working of such Company.

A Private Limited Company is formed by a minimum of two members with a maximum of 50 (fifty) members. Its shares cannot be transferred freely. Such a Company is also prohibited from inviting the public to subscribe to its shares or debentures. Private Limited Companies are, however, not subject to all the regulatory provisions which are applicable to Public Limited Companies.

Q. 28. Is it of necessity that there should be interaction between the superior officers of the Organisations and the staff members?

Ans. Yes, there should be interaction between the superior officers remaining at the helm of affairs of the Organisation and the staff members. Concept of working in establishments has completely changed in modern times. Master and servant relations are no longer there in the Organisations. All employees, whether high or low, have to work unitedly for the Organisation and each and every employee has his contribution to render for the development and prosperity of the Organisation. If barriers are there between the superior officers at the helm of affairs and the staff members generating feelings of superiority and inferiority complex working under the same roof, sense of belongings to the Organisation by the staff members will be conspicuous by its absence which will be an impediment for the development and prosperity of the Organisation. At the same time, it is of course very necessary that while working unitedly by the superior officers and the staff members, maintenance of difference in their official positions should be maintained. Otherwise, it will lead to indiscipline.

Work will be speeded up if the staff members are given due importance and prestige no matter their salaries may be much lesser than those of the officers of the Company. Generation of oneness has to be created. Therefore, interaction between the superior officers at the helm of affairs and the staff members is essentially needed in consideration of the fact that all the employees are the members of the same family. By this, sweet and cordial relations between the officers and the staff members will also be maintained.

Q. 29. What is the distinctive function of Managing Director and Director?

Ans. The Managing Director has to play the role of Chief Executive of the Company. So, he has to perform those functions which are normally performed by the Chief Executive. He is the Director in one hand and Manager on the other. Whereas, an individual Director has no power and authority in the affairs of the Company. He has to act collectively through resolutions passed at the meeting of the Board. He is the representative of the shareholders. Directors are the policy makers.

Q. 30. Can a charge-sheeted employee engage a lawyer to defend himself in the disciplinary proceedings?

Ans. Management is not to abide by the request of the delinquent employee to engage a lawyer to defend his case, if the prosecution officer on behalf of the Company is not legally trained. In such case, the charge-sheeted employee cannot claim to be defended by a lawyer as a matter of right. If, however, the prosecution officer is legally trained, the delinquent employee can also engage a legal professional to defend his case in the enquiry proceedings and in that case the Management cannot have any objection.

Q. 31. Is it in order that the Management could impose punishment to a delinquent employee on the basis of the findings of the Enquiry Officer in the domestic enquiry?

Ans. Domestic enquiry is a court where findings are arrived at to judge whether the concerned employee is actually at fault or not in the matter of charges levelled against him by the Management. It is, therefore, perfectly in order that the Management can act upon the judgement of the Enquiry Officer in awarding punishment to a delinquent employee if the charges are proved against him in the domestic enquiry. The Supreme Court of India has also laid down that where a disciplinary authority states that he has gone into the findings of the Enquiry Officer and agrees with the same, it is sufficient that the Management can go ahead with inflicting punishment if the charges are substantiated in the domestic enquiry conducted by the Enquiry Officer. There is of course provision that the aggrieved employee can challenge the orders of the Management by way of writ application in the appropriate High Court.

Q. 32. If a Labour Court awards only 50 per cent of back wages to an employee who was reinstated from dismissal of his services on account of the principles of natural justice, can he claim full back wages on his reinstatement?

Ans. The law is that the dismissed employee on reinstatement may not be entitled to get full back wages. The decision of the Labour Court to award 50 per cent of back wages depends upon the facts and circumstances of each case. From the normality point of view, the high court will also not interfere with the quantum of back wages awarded by the Labour Court. If, however, the reinstated employee feels that it was unreasonable on the part of the labour court to award only 50 per cent of back wages, he can challenge the award of the labour court before the appropriate High Court in its writ jurisdiction.

Q. 33. It may so happen in the office that an employee working under a departmental head is not allotted any work by him thereby putting him practically without work for which the employee starts feeling humiliated in the eye of others, which is the result of some hitch developed with his departmental head. In such case, can the employee take legal course to get out of the impasse?

Ans. As far as employee-employer relation is concerned, it is entirely the discretion of the departmental head to distribute work. If an employee is not allotted work and he continues to get salary, as usual even if he is made to sit idle in the office without being allotted any work, he does not have any recourse left for him to redress his grievances against the departmental head.

On the issue of humiliation the concerned employee should try to sort out the problem through discussions with the HRD personnel or the higher Management.

Q. 34. What are the criteria by which employees get job satisfaction?

Ans. Job satisfaction is a very important factor which leads employees attaining their efficiency in working and the Organisation in turn is also benefitted much by getting the efficient services of the employees. Hence, job satisfaction has dual advantages. There are number of important factors by which employees can get job satisfaction. They are—congenial atmosphere in the office, cordial relationship between the management and the employees, standardisation in the salary structure compatible with the cost of living index and the paying capacity of the Organisation, right job for the right employees, allowing attractive fringe benefits depending upon the status of the Organisation, so that the employees are devoted to work which will breed work culture and the provision for promotion of employees.

Q. 35. What are Holding and Subsidiary Companies? What is the difference between the two?

Ans. When a Company has control over another Company, it is known as Holding Company and the Company so controlled by the Holding Company is called a Subsidiary Company.

The analyses of the Subsidiary Company are as follows:

(i) When the composition of the Board of Directors of the Company is controlled by another company, it is a Subsidiary Company.

(ii) When the majority of the shares of the Company is held by another Company, it is a Subsidiary Company.

Q. 36. Can a confirmed employee submit resignation with less than thirty days notice?

Ans. A confirmed employee is a regular employee of an Organisation. In terms of appointment letter/Service Agreement he has to submit 30 days/90 days notice, as the case may be, while submitting his letter of resignation. If, however, such employee wants to resign with less than 30 days/90 days notice, he can do so and in that case the number of days which fall short of the notice period will be adjusted from his accumulated earned leave salary/bonus payable to him. If the number of days falling short of notice period does not even cover the accumulated leave salary/bonus payable to him, the employee has to pay the amount from his own pocket before he is released from service. In this connexion, it may be noted that the Provident Fund amount cannot be attached to cover the shortfall of the number of days of notice period.

Q. 37. Should the employees resort to gheraos to the officials of Organisations in the event of not fulfilling the demands of the employees backed by the Labour Union?

Ans. It is likely that there may be discord between the employees, duly backed by the Union leaders and the Management over non-fulfilling of the demands of the employees by the Management. In such case, militant and arrogant attitude enticing the employers by way of resorting to gheraos should not be adopted by the employees to agree to their sky-rocketing demands. This is not the democratic way of getting things resolved, which will have far-reaching adverse consequences. Employees should bear in mind that employers always enjoy upper hand. Settlement of matters across the table in an atmosphere of cordiality and give-and-take is always welcome. This way employee-employer relations will also continue to be maintained which is of paramount necessity. Employees should take into congnisance as to how things are resolved in commercial establishments in Japan which is a progressive and prosperous industrial nation in the world. Employees there never resort to strike, gheraos and/or cause to suffer production, but in a disciplined way they show their resentment over non-fulfilling of issues, by wearing black badges for settlement of disputed matters by the Management. Employees working in Indian Organisations should also follow suit of the Japanese methods of settlement of things. The prime objective of the employees should be to see that Organisations in which they are employed run undisturbed.

Q. 38. On the first day of reporting to duties what should be the role of the employees?

Ans. First day of attendance of an employee to an Organisation testifies his capacity of quick adjustment in the new environment. A new employee feels easy when he has adjustment capacity, which is very important for the employees. It may so happen that a few of the existing employees may not extend their hands of cooperation to a new entrant. In such case, he can woo their hearts by his pleasing manners and soft attitude. This is very necessary that a new employee has to seek the help of the existing employees to know about the system of working at the initial stage even if he may be an experienced hand.

Punctuality in attendance of the employee is of absolute necessity. He should be neat and clean in his well-fitted attire. His first duty will be to report to his departmental head and submit his joining report. It is the usual practice that a new employee is got introduced with the co-employees by the departmental head/or senior most employee of the department.

The language of the joining report letter will be in the following lines:

____________ Date ____________

____

Sir,

Re : Joining Report

Apropos your letter of appointment bearing No. ________ dated ________offering me the post of __________ in your esteemed Organisation/ your informing me on 'phone about my appointment in your esteemed Organisation in the capacity of______?,' I hereby report on duty this forenoon, the ________ (mention date).

Thanking you,

Yours faithfully,

____

N.B.

The joining report letter should be addressed to the issuing authority of appointment letter and is to be submitted to Departmental head.

Q. 39. When an employee starts losing interest in job, what steps should he adopt to rejuvenate his working spirit?

Ans. There are number of factors responsible for eroding interest in the working of an employee who ought to be in the know of the same before he takes steps to rejuvenate his working spirit. The following are the probable reasons of losing interest in working:

(a) Lack of enthusiasm to rise high in service tends to have impact in eroding interest in working.

(b) It is the general tendency of the employees that when they are under the shadow of labour union they nurture the conception that they are protected employees, even if they do not work sincerely for the Organisation. This leads to dwindling of their interest in working in most of the cases.

(c) Ease loving and lethargic employees are lacking in interest in working.

(d) If there is no prospect of development of employees' future in the Organisation, interest in working becomes on the wane.

(e) Adverse family atmosphere of the employees plays an important part in drying up interest in working.

(f) Working in incongenial atmosphere in office tends to wither interest in working.

Losing interest in working will dampen the prospect of the employees to rise high in service. Whatever may be the reasons for losing interest in working, the employees should take the following steps to rejuvenate their working spirit in their own interest.

(a) Employees should set aside time for self-developmental activities.

(b) Explore possibilities for further studies.

(c) Make time to be with the members of their families and discuss matters of interest.

(d) Devote more time to their hobbies.

(e) Go for week-end trips and get themselves involved in social work.

(f) Try to be free from scarce and anxieties.

(g) Mixing up with people with free mind.

(h) Mind should be kept light always.

Q. 40. Can employees withdraw amount from their Public Provident Fund (PPF) before completion of five years of contributing to the Fund?

Ans. Under Section 6(1) of the Public Provident Fund (PPF) Act, 1968, a subscriber shall be entitled to make withdrawal from the amount standing to his credit in the fund to such extent and subject to such terms and conditions as may be specified in the PPF Scheme, but only after the expiry of a period of five years from the end of the year in which he made the initial subscription. However, the employee may apply for a loan out of the amount standing to his credit in the fund and the authority may under Section-7 of the PPF Act grant such loan on such terms and conditions, as may be specified in the PPF Scheme.

It is also for the information of the employees that they can unconditionally withdraw the entire balance standing to their credit in the fund after expiry of 15 years from the end of the year in which they made the initial subscription to the PPF as provided in Section 6(2) of the Act.

Q. 41. What is meant by 'front office activity,' and 'back office activity'?

Ans. For the purpose of convenience of working, some employees are engaged in front office activity depending upon their certain qualitative aspects. These employees come in contact with clients and customers through letters, telephones, personal visits or meeting at any place. On the other hand, employees engaged in back office activity give support service to front office personnel and they do not come in contact with the clients and customers, as in the case of the employees engaged in front office activity.

Q. 42. A few of the employees while attending to duties to a new Organisation continue to suffer from trepidation for a number of days. Why?

Ans. This is happening mostly with the inexperienced employees who have just started their service career. They are not in fact habituated to work in unison by mingling with the different categories of employees. They suffer unnecessarily from fear psychosis, which is the result of their being practically fresh in service. These employees are under the impression that they will be at fault while doing work of the Organisation and that their departmental heads will start taking sneering attitude on them from the very beginning of their service. They suffer from nervousness and feel difficulty to adjust themselves with the new situation.

What are the solutions to get rid of this fear, psychosis and trepidation? Remedies are clear-cut based on the following:

(a) When the employees have made impressive performance in interviews for which they have been employed in the Organisations, this is their greatest satisfaction that they are to the liking of the management. Obviously, this will add strength to them to begin working without fear psychosis and trepidation.

(b) For the new employees freeness of mind and adaptability to the new situation are very important to begin with the working with calm and ease.

(c) The employees must be rapacious to know the system of working by asking the co-employees and the departmental heads for clarifications, when needed,

(d) They must ensure that the work done by them is all with perfection, no matter they may be slow in doing the work at the initial stage.

(e) The employees must not show that they are ruffled or fluttered while at work.

Q. 43. What are the ways as to how an employee has to exhibit respectability to his superior officers?

Ans. It is incumbent on the part of each and every employee to exhibit respectability to his superior officers. This will deepen affection towards the employees and the work of Organisations will be carried on in peaceful environment. Showing disrespect by an employee to his superior officers by way of disobedience, disloyalty, obstinacy and unbecoming way of talking is the evidence that he is indisciplined. Such employee spoils the working atmosphere and sanctity of office is seriously impaired. This situation should under no circumstances be allowed to crop up.

The following are the ways as to how an employee has to exhibit respectability to his superior officers:

(a) It is not necessary that an employee is to be a 'yes' man always with the purpose of satisfying his superior officers. This proves that such employee wants to get undue favour through his oily tongue. This is a wrong conception on the part of an employee which should be eschewed.

(b) Performing duties in pursuance of instructions from superior officers is a way of showing respectability.

(c) Although there is interaction between the employees and the superior officers which ensures freeness of working with affinity in relation between the employees and the superior officers, the employees in any case must show respect to the chair by way of obeisance.

(d) No employee has to enter into contradiction with superior officers at any time.

(e) Talking in submissive way but with straightforwardness is another way of showing respectability to the superior officers.

(f) Discharging duties fully by the employees assigned to them is also a way to show respectability to the superior officers.

(g) Another way of showing respectability by the employee is that he has to give due information to his superior officer while leaving the office for the day that the job allotted to him could not be completed because of complication/cumbrousness of the same and that it would be completed in cool brain in the very first hour of next day. Non-informing the same by the employee shows his disregard to his superior officer.

Q. 44. Should the employees go on changing Organisations frequently?

Ans. Changing Organisations frequently does not speak high of an employee as also his stable mind. While going for interviews by an employee the interviewers are of the opinion that with such habit the employee may not stick to the job after his appointment and that they have to make advertisements again for filling up the vacancy. The effect of switching over to different companies by an employee is that his chance of getting employment dries up in many cases, as the employers are not generally willing to appoint employee with such habit. Another important point is that for the purpose of qualifying for entitlement of gratuity payment an employee has to put in service in a particular Organisation uninterruptedly for five years; but if the employee goes on changing Organisations before completion of five years service there, he will be debarred from getting gratuity which is no doubt a substantial amount.

For a new employee changing job initially is of course necessary with the purpose of gleaning wide experience, which will be to his advantage of getting employment in other Organisations. But, if the employee feels that he is well set in such Organisation and his continuity in service will benefit him, he should not think of switch-over.

It is always recommended that no employee should think of changing a good Company. But, of course in exceptional cases taking into consideration broader perspective, an experienced employee may switch over to other Organisations even before completion of five years continuous service. Also there are many small Organisations where no perks and fringe benefits are given to the employees excepting salary only and standing of such Organisations is unstable. In such case, the employees should seek better chance of employment elsewhere, as their future in such Organisations is blocked.

Q. 45. During the course of working an employee may be fired by his superior officer for the wrongs committed by him. In such case, what should be his reaction?

Ans. There is a saying, "To Err is Human." But, it does not mean that an employee will go on committing mistakes in his working always. Committing mistakes frequently is the manifestation that the employee does not work with steady mind. Minor mistakes committed by him and that too not frequently is of course tolerable. It is but natural that the superior officer is likely to be enraged when an employee continues to commit mistakes in his working repeatedly and fires on him. Firing on the employee by his superior officer is definitely a benediction in disguise and the employee must not pull a long face for such firing which is done for the alertness and rectification of the employee in his working in future. An employee must always bear in mind that such firing is necessary for his good and that he will be perfect in his working in future. Also the employee must not at all think of bearing ill-feeling towards his superior officer for such firing. If done so, it will simply display his unsteady, weak and touchy mind which will adversely affect his service career.

Q. 46. What are the ways an employee can impress upon his superior officers?

Ans. It should be the objective of each and every employee that he should impress upon his superior officers by way of his maintaining decorum and other aspects which include the following:

(a) An employee has to take care of that he maintains punctuality in his attendance.

(b) He must give due respect to the chair and be obedient to his superior officer.

(c) He must work with sincerity and full devotion.

(d) He must keep the work up-to-date.

(e) He should maintain cordial relations with his co-employees and other officers of the Company.

(f) He should be cooperative with his colleagues.

(g) He should abstain from taking leave every now and then.

(h) He should be submissive in his manners and behaviour.

(i) He should be disciplined.

(j) He should not be a clock watcher while leaving office for the day.

Q. 47. What are the other factors which help employees ascend to higher position in service?

Ans. Apart from what has been discussed earlier in this book in respect of the ingredients needed for ascending to high position in service by employees, another important aspect is that it should be the endeavour of the employees to prosecute studies in management and secretarial practice which are likely to give them an overview of the corporate and business world with good communication skills and computer knowledge.

If the same could be attained apart from acquiring the ingredients as already analysed, the employees will get impetus to work with further zeal and enthusiasm and the prospect of their promotion in service will be brightened and hastened.

Q. 48. An employee aspiring to work in managerial capacity must have knowledge of correspondence in English. How to glean knowledge of doing correspondence?

Ans. Knowledge of correspondence is an essential part to work in managerial capacity. An employee aspiring to work in the said position must have knowledge how to make independent correspondence in English which is mostly used in commercial enterprises. Without comfortable knowledge of English it will not be possible on the part of an employee to make correspondence. Language is the conveyor of what is to be expressed. In order, therefore, to master the art of independent correspondence, an employee has to get himself conversant with the following:

(a) He has to develop at least comfortable knowledge of English so that the matters which are to be conveyed at the other end could be expressed in official language which should be simple and easy to understand. Verbose style of English in official correspondence is to be avoided.

(b) The matters to be written in correspondence should be to the point and concise. Unnecessary lengthy correspondence which irks the executives in going through it is not desirable. He is a busy person and he has no time to go through such lengthy letters.

(c) Conception of working is very important in making correspondence which means what is required to be expressed on the basis of conception of working. Without conception nothing can be expressed in letters. Making flawless and standard correspondence augments the prestige and reputation of an Organisation.

(d) The best way to know the style and mode of correspondence is to go through the relevant office files in which number of copies of different types of correspondence have been filed. It is advisable that before going through the files consent of the senior officers is obtained, wherever necessary. In such case, this decorum has to be followed.

Habit of making correspondence in the above manner is to be practised and maturity in the same will be attained in the not too distant future.

Q. 49. Do the employees need protection of labour union for working in Organisations?

Ans. As per Indian Constitution Trade Unionism is a right of the employees. Hence, there is no wrong if there should be labour union in any Organisation. It is the objective of labour union to ensure right cause for the employees. The purpose of labour union is to act as the go-between the management and the employees mainly in matters of maintaining employee-employer relations, rational way of fixation of salary structure commensurate to the size and financial standing of Organisations, up-keep of congenial working atmosphere, fixation of percentage of bonus payable to the employees, maintaining productivity of the organisations etc.

It is an admitted fact that no enlightened management becomes irrational in dealing with their employees. Still then it has been observed that in most of the cases employees forming labour union or under its tutelage resort to work to rule leaving office sharp at the end of office timing—no matter the work entrusted with them has been completed or not and adopt other delatory process. The employees have the conception that they are protected by the union and that their services can never be at stake.

Labour union has never educated the employees to work to rule which is not a healthy sign of progress and development of Organisations. Growth of employees has direct link with the growth of Organisations. Therefore, it should be the joint responsibility of both the management and the employees backed by the union to work for the progress and development of Organisations—no matter the employees are under the umbrella of labour union. Organisations have come to stay and not to get them wound up which should be upheld. Labour union should see that Organisations run undisturbed for the protection of the employees and that there should be unison between the management and the employees.

Q. 50. Can an employee refuse acceptance of letter of charge-sheet issued by the Management?

Ans. It is not desirable on the part of an employee to refuse acceptance of letter of charge-sheet issued to him by the Management. Even if he refuses acceptance of the same, there will be no escape for him for non-acceptance of such letter. In this case, as per official norm the management will display the letter of charge-sheet in their notice board with the remark, "In the event of non-acceptance of this letter by the employee, it is being displayed in the notice board." While displaying such letter in the notice board, the management will put names of two of its employees with their signatures on the letter in question as witness. This way of displaying the letter in the notice board is as good as serving the same to the erring employee.

It is, therefore, suggested that no employee should refuse acceptance of letter of charge-sheet or any other letter issued by the management, else it will unnecessarily strain relation with the management, which must be avoided always.

Q. 51. Should an employee think of quitting employment in view, of the fact that his salary is lesser than that of his contemporary co-employee having been appointed in the same year, although the nature of work of both of them is the same and that he has been working with sincerity and undertaking more load of work than his co-employee?

Ans. In such case, quitting employment will not bring solution to problem of the aggrieved employee, rather it is likely to precipitate the same provided no lucrative offer from other Organisation is available in his hands at the same time. More so, if the Organisation where he has been working is quite reputable and has good standing in the country, hasty decision to quit the employment on this count will be nothing but foolishness. This will also prove his unsteady mind, which does not speak well of his servitude mind. Under the circumstances, the best course left for him will be to discuss about the cause of his dissatisfaction in the matter of difference in salary, with his immediate superior officer so as to get his assurance of redressal of grievance. While discussing the matter with him the aggrieved employee will also be in a position to know the assessment of the superior officer about his (employee's) workability and his usefulness to the Organisation.

If nothing tangible happens after discussing the matter with him, the employee may then decide his own course of action in the matter of sticking to the Organisation, if he feels that difference in salary will render him inefficient and his working spirit will dwindle.

Q. 52. What is work culture of an employee?

Ans. Work culture means consciousness of working *i.e.* eagerness of an employee to perform work with diligence and sincerity. An employee with dereliction of work culture cannot thrive in service. An ambitious employee must not have servitude mindedness. While working for the Organisation for which he has been appointed he should think that it is his own work. For attaining work culture an employee must not give bluff to the work entrusted to him. An employee possessing work culture is to yearn to hit the road to success, which should be his intense purpose. He should have voracity to work. Punctuality in his attendance to office is the reflection that he believes in work culture. An employee possessing work culture feels uneasy to waste time. He is devotional to work always. For him work is worship.

Q. 53. How could the employees develop knowledge of English —both spoken and written, which is essentially needed to construct road to ascend to high position in service?

Ans. In the present-day education system most of the adolescents, barring aside those educated from English medium schools, are not adept in English even though they are graduates. Reasons for the same are not far to seek which are stated briefly, as follows:

(a) Unnecessary fear psychosis to learn English has generated in their minds.

(b) Many of them have tendency to pass examinations in English after committing to memories/the lessons which are likely to be found common in examinations.

(c) Foundation of knowledge of English has been made weak on account of improper and archaic guidance of teacher.

(d) Lack of devotion to learn English.

Following are the suggestions as to how to develop knowledge of English:

(a) First of all, fear psychosis to learn English has to be dispelled from minds. It is to be borne in mind that because of popularity of this language it has become a *lingua franca* and that it is not at all a tough language to learn.

(b) Habit of reading English newspaper regularly will help a lot to learn English. At the initial stage the readers may feel difficulty to understand meanings, as they may not be accustomed with many words and their uses. They should prefer to read such English newspaper which is easy in expressions.

(c) They should have common grammatical knowledge so as to enable them to construct sentences correctly. Such book of good writer available in the market should be gone through.

(d) They should abjure inclination to learn verbose style of English which will torment their minds, rather they should have leaning towards learning simple English.

(e) Employees should make a habit to converse in English with their colleagues most of the time, although there may be mistakes in speaking at the initial stage.

None of the employees who are deficient in the knowledge of English should expect that they could be adept in English overnight. Systematic practice, as suggested, will surely help them learn English in the not too distant future and that they will have additional strength and confidence to shoulder higher job responsibilities.

Q. 54. Why does an employee need basic English background to work in managerial position?

Ans. Periphery of working of an officer dealing with managerial functions is widened manifold. Apart from working within the four walls of office, he has also to mingle intimately and deal with galaxy of intellectuals and executives of different Organisation for business and other purposes.

Executives of Organisations and government officials are generally hailing from different states, whose mother tongues are not similar to one another. Hence, use of common language is of absolute necessity to converse with them. Knowledge of English being the common language for the educated persons of different states of India is felt an absolute necessity by the employees aspiring for ascending to managerial positions for the purpose of maintaining business relations and also close acquaintances as well as intimacy with others, which is one of the important functions of a Manager. Therefore, the prospective employees must have excellent written and communication skills, which need proficiency in English for working in Managerial position. Also sound knowledge of English is absolutely necessary to make variegated types of correspondence. The employees should start preparing themselves to get them conversant with the art of doing independent correspondence in English before they are elevated to the managerial positions.

Q. 55. In an Organisation there is the conglomeration of employees with different caste and creed working for the common cause. Under the circumstances, should there be any community feeling and difference in dealings from one and the other on this count?

Ans. Community feeling in office, if there be any, is a bane which must not be allowed to dawn under any circumstances in the minds of the employees. Otherwise, it will have serious repercussion in the smooth working of the Organisation. Dormant community feeling leads to non-cooperation of the employees which adversely affects the working. Employees have to bear in mind that India is a unity in diversity and every person has equal rights and status in the comity of nations. There should be pleasure to work amongst the employees with different caste and creed. Needless to mention, for a big country like India an Organisation is a house accommodating heterogeneity of employees hailing from different states and it becomes an opportunity to mingle and work together with such employees in one platform. Bearing ill-feeling towards one another is a manifestation of parochialism which does not augur well of an employee. Such employee cannot have broadness of mind. Broadness of mind is of course absolutely necessary to work in high position; because a senior officer/Manager has to work with galaxy of employees with different caste and creed and showing of community feeling, provincialism as well as any partiality in his treatment and dealings will never show high of him and he will be unsuccessful in his working in managerial capacity. Employees should, therefore, ensure that they have their broadness of mind without any community feeling and provincialism.

Q. 56. During the course of working when an employee faces some complicated work, what should he do?

Ans. It is obvious that an employee cannot have plain sailing in his working all the times. During the course of working he must be prepared to face complicated work also. In such circumstances, his worriness and perplexity of mind will further worsen the situation and he will be completely confused to solve the problem. The best course left for the employee will be to have patience, steadiness and undisturbed mind. Experience of an employee will be deep-seated when he becomes habituated to handle complicated work. In dealing with complicated work there should not be any time factor that such job has to be done with perfection within the limited and specified time. Working against time will complicate the job further. Deep concentration of mind while at work is an absolute necessity. If the employee feels that such complicated work cannot be accomplished without the help of others, he should seek guidance from his departmental head without fail.

Under any circumstances, the employee must not be ruffled in temperament while dealing with complicated work. Otherwise, solution to such problematic work will not be a fruition. He has to bear in mind that facing complicated work by him time to time is a test of his steady and unshaking mind without which he is not expected of shouldering higher responsibilities in service.

Q. 57. During the course of employment when an employee loses confidence of the higher management, what is the course left for him under the circumstances?

Ans. It is a fact that when the higher management loses confidence of an employee it is no doubt a hard task on his part to rebuild it. Losing confidence of an employee slanders his image. When an employee has to work in an Organisation with honour and prestige, he must ensure that he is always in the good books of the higher management. Otherwise, there will be no sense to continue in employment with the Organisation any longer, as the higher management will find its way that the concerned employee is compelled to quit employment.

There are a number of reasons as to why the higher management loses confidence of an employee which may be summarised, as follows:

Confidence is lost—

(a) When an employee does not come to the expectation of the higher management in the discharge of his duties assigned to him. This is on account of laxity of the employee.

(b) When an employee is insincere in his duties.

(c) When he has no sense of respectability towards his superior officers.

(d) When he is in the habit of criticising his superior officer—both his working and on his personal matters.

(e) When he has argumentive habits.

(f) When he has no sense of etiquette.

(g) When he has no love for work.

The above are the shortcomings of an employee which hold the onus of responsibility for incurring wrath of the higher management which in effect tends to losing confidence of the employee.

When all the above are the negative sides of an employee depriving him of the confidence of the higher management, it should be his utmost endeavour to regain confidence by not indulging in the commission of the afore-said shortcomings. The higher management will also start realising that good sense has prevailed upon the employee in rectifying himself to become a perfect and upright employee in all respects. If, however, he fails to amend himself the only course left for him is to quit employment, as such employee has no place in the Organisation.

Q. 58. Supposing, the post in which an employee has been working stands abolished and consequently the services of the employee are terminated. Can the employee challenge his termination in the court of law on the plea that he was not given any hearing before termination of his services?

Ans. Due to exigency of circumstances, abolition of any post is a matter of policy of higher management. Accordingly, the consequential termination of services of the employee is not dismissal. In this connexion, the court has given ruling that it is not compulsorily necessary on the part of higher management to give any opportunity of hearing to the incumbent before abolition of the post. Arising out of necessity, the higher management of an Organisation can create new posts and also wind up the same. Therefore, the court will not interfere in the matter relating to abolition of post unless it is arbitrary and malafide or is a pretext for dismissal of the employee. In view of the above, no purpose will be served if the aggrieved employee takes recourse to the court of law for redressal.

If, however, the higher management would be in a comfortable position to accommodate such employee in some other post, it will be a case of fresh employment and the continuity in service will not be reckoned.

Q. 59. Can an Organisation withhold payment of dues of an employee who has resigned from services on the ground of financial stringency?

Ans. As a matter of fact, no Organisation can withhold legitimate dues of an employee who has resigned from the services, on the ground of financial stringency. It will also not be proper on the part of the Organisation to tell the ex-employee that his dues will be cleared after receipt of outstanding amount from other Organisation/s which may be received in the near future, which is of course uncertain. The concerned employee can ill afford to bear such uncertain situation for unnamed period. Under the circumstances, the employee can file a civil suit against the Organisation at their costs and expenses under Section 434 of the Companies Act, 1956 for recovery of his dues.

Q. 60. For speedy rise in service career an employee must have both CQ and IQ. How these two essential ingredients are explained?

Ans. 'CQ' stands for Contemporary Quotient and that 'IQ' Intelligence Quotient. In order to develop 'CQ' an employee has to acquaint, himself thoroughly with pretty much everything, all around. Intelligence Quotient is the skill of logical reasoning, problem solving capacity, critical thinking and adaptation. The employees who are smart and serious in their working can acquire these two ingredients quickly. Working in meaningful way is the incarnation of possessing Intelligence Quotient. Employees taking part in fruitful and fertile discussions amongst their colleagues can also broaden their Intelligence Quotient. Perfection in the working is ensured by the employees possessing both CQ and IQ. Development of both Contemporary Quotient and Intelligence Quotient is very important for the employees to create good impression in the minds of the superior officers.

Q. 61. When an employee attains fairly good experience of working, what should be his dealings and attitude towards his boss?

Ans. • When an employee by virtue of his concerted and sincere efforts gleans fairly good experience of working in the department, it will be his utter foolishness if he defies his boss obsessed with the wrong conception that he is no less inferior to him in the matter of working. Also he must not enter into confrontation with his boss at any point of time and show his disloyalty and untrustworthiness to him. It is good that the employee by his IQ and hard working has reached a turning point when his case for promotion has become the subject of discussion of the higher management. In such situation, it will be prudent on the part of the employee that he should be more submissive and loyal to his boss so that the affinity in the relation between the employee and the boss is strengthened further. It may so happen that the qualification of the boss is equal or a bit lower than that of the employee's but in such case also the employee must show due regards to his boss, because the chair has respectability which is not measured in terms of qualifications of the person who occupies it.

Q. 62. If the cheque issued by the official of the company to an ex-employee in full and final settlement of his dues is bounced, what is the course left for him in such situation?

Ans. It is not at all correct on the part of the official to issue cheque under his signature to an ex-employee in full and final settlement of his dues when it is known to him that the cheque in question when presented to the bank will be bounced on account of shortage of balance in the account of the Company. This is no doubt a criminal offence of the concerned official issuing the cheque. However, in the event of bouncing of the cheque, the ex-employee can take the following actions:

(a) When validity of the non-governmental cheque is for six months from the date of its issue the same can be presented to the bank again after it was bounced earlier, within its validity period for encashment.

(b) This time also if the cheque is dishonoured a demand notice in writing must be served on the official issuing the cheque within 30 days of the date of information of the bouncing.

(c) After receiving the demand notice if the concerned official of the Company still fails to pay the amount to the ex-employee within 15 days of receiving such notice, a criminal complaint can be filed in the court of law by the ex-employee within one month from that date.

Incidentally, it may be mentioned that the ex-employee should not accept any post-dated cheque, as after ceasing the employee-employer relations on the very date of his release from the services of the Company, he cannot afford to wait for another number of days for encashment of the cheque, if it is of course honoured by that time.

Q. 63. When an employee has to discuss some official matters with his superior officer in his office chamber, what propriety or decorum has to be maintained by him?

Ans. Maintenance of propriety or decorum by a disciplined employee while discussing official matters with his superior officer is absolutely necessary. This speaks of uprightness of the employee. It will not look nice if an employee sits straightway in the chair placed across the desk of the superior officer before he is asked to take his seat. If done so, this displays a bit of arrogance and intemperance and also lack of etiquette and modesty of the employee. While discussing matters the employee has to listen to with rapt attention what the superior officer explains to him. While listening to the explanations of the superior officer, the employee should maintain eye contact with his boss. He should not also interfere by telling his own points of argument during the course of explaining matters. Showing submissiveness by the employee to his superior officer will help his boss to be free with the employee and the affinity in the relations between the superior officer and the employee will be maintained by such submissiveness.

Q. 64. What should be the relation between a staff member and a superior officer outside office premises?

Ans. Employees/staff members are inseparable from Organisation. They are part and parcel of it. Superior officers/Departmental heads/Managers are to work in collaboration with the staff members. Every employee has his own responsibility to perform in an Organisation and hence his working is not less important in line with his official position. Bossism of course is to be maintained in the office by the staff members/employees. Even if office hours are over and both the employees and the superior officers are still working in the office, bossism has to be kept up for the sake of upholding discipline in the Organisation.

Outside office premises the question of bossism should not be there. But, it does not mean that both staff members/employees and the superior officers have to walk shoulder to shoulder catching hold of both of them. If the superior officers nurture the conception that they are still bosses of the employees outside office premises also, it does not speak high of them and the employees will not feel easy to commune with them. Outside office premises official matters are not to be discussed because the same is not the actual forum for such topics for discussion. When freeness in the relations between the senior officers and staff members is upheld outside office premises, inclination to working is deepened by the employees in the office. This is a psychological point of view. It is, therefore, always in the fitness of things that barriers of bossism are removed outside office premises and there should be freeness in their relations. Relations amongst them in the office and outside are different aspects and these are not to be equated.

Q. 65. After returning back home from office by an employee in the evening, what should he do?

Ans. After toiling hard in the office when an employee returns back home in the evening, he must dispel tension from his mind and will remain free from all scarce and anxieties. He should also keep himself jovial and look pleasant. When the work in the office is a daily affair, it does not mean that his mind will be obsessed with the thinking of official work even after returning back home. If he does so, he will start becoming ruffled in temperament which will affect his working next day in the office. After coming back home he will naturally feel relieved and this relief becomes a refreshment to him which will rejuvenate him to work with full of enthusiasm in the office next day and he will never feel exhaustion in the discharge of his duties. If the employee is unmarried he should after taking a bit of rest and refreshment mix up with his friends in his locality or go to the club in the vicinity of his residence to be with his friends and play indoor games there. If the employee is married he should give company to the members of his family and watch T.V. programmes together with them. It is the expectation of the members of his family that he should give close company to them after long absence from home. This will deepen his family ties. No member of his family wants that his working in the office will make him mechanised being oblivious of family needs and problems.

Q. 66. If the employer/senior officer asks any employee to do outside work every now and then in addition to his indoor work, will he show his unwillingness to do the same?

Ans. Non-compliance of reasonable orders of employer/ senior officer by an employee is misconduct on his part. Of course, there is no wrong to refuse doing outside work and that too in a polite manner by the employee, if it is derogatory to his official status. When an employee is accustomed to perform outside work in line with his official status apart from doing indoor work, his experience of working will be pretty high. During the course of doing outside work, he gets immense opportunity to come in contact with different strata of people which will help him know human sentiments and behaviours. While doing outside work he must be polite and amenable so that he does not face rebuff to accomplish the work assigned to him. The higher management will no doubt eulogise him when he attains success in achieving results. This will be his plus point as an employee. Performing work—both indoor and outdoor by an employee with perfection will push him up in his employment with the Organisation.

Q. 67. When an employee feels fatigue and clumsy while continuing to work constantly in the office, what should he do?

Ans. In such situation, the only panacea is to have freeness of mind. It is but natural that on account of constant work fatigue and clumsiness are bound to come to an employee and he must find his way to get out of the same so as to enable him to perform the work of which he is engaged, with perfection. When the employee starts feeling fatigue and clumsy owing to devotion to duties constantly, he should give a pause to his work for a short while and freshen his mind by diverting his attention to other aspect not related to work of the office. Under such situation, the best course will be to have a cup of tea which will help him dispel fatigue and clumsiness. Apart from this, it will also be better to repose in his seat for a little while and consequently he will regain freeness of mind. Work performed with freeness of mind becomes flawless. Employees must ensure that their efficiency in working does not dwindle on account of fatigue and clumsiness which could be removed by the above methods during the course of working.

Q. 68. If the services of an employee, who was appointed in an organisation without any appointment letter, are dispensed with without any reason and prior notice, can he get back his job by filing any legal proceeding?

Ans. Engagement of a person without issuing any appointment letter to him by an Organisation is similar to that of a personal service, which has no *locus standi* in the eye of law. Appointment of an employee against issuance of appointment letter has relevance of law governing the following and the employee can go for taking legal action if his services are dispensed with in contravention of law.

(a) Where an employee is sought to be removed from service in contravention of Article 311 of the Constitution.

(b) Where a dismissed employee is sought to be reinstated under the Industrial Disputes Act, 1947.

(c) Where a statutory body dismisses an employee in violation of any mandatory provision of the relevant Statute.

Therefore, any legal proceeding an employee without any appointment letter may file is not likely to succeed.

Q. 69. What are Unfair Labour Practices (ULP) resorted to by the workmen and registered Trade Unions?

Ans. Section 2(ra) of the Industrial Disputes Act, 1947 states that "Unfair Labour Practice" means any of the practices specified in the Fifth Schedule to the Act. Part-II of the said Schedule specifies the acts which amount to unfair labour practices on the part of the workmen or their Trade Union, which are as follows:

(i) To advise or actively support or instigate any strike deemed to be illegal under the act.

(ii) To stage demonstrations at the residences of the employers or the managerial staff.

(iii) To indulge in acts of violence against any workman to obstruct him from attending work.

Under Section 25 (U) of the Industrial Disputes Act, 1947, any workman belonging to registered Trade Union committing any of the above acts, duly supported by them (Union) shall be punishable with imprisonment for a period of six months or with fine upto Rs. 1,000 or with both.

Q. 70. How to work by an employee with a boss who is very tough and maintains gravity all the times in the office?

Ans. From the psychological point of view, employees working under a boss who is very tough and maintains gravity all the times in the office feel hesitant to be frequent with him. Conception of such officer is that if the employees are frequent to him, his own way of working will not be smooth and that he will fail to do justice to the higher management by his judicious decisions on certain intricate matters. In order, therefore, to restrict frequency to him by the employees working under him, he has the slip system for them and the employees are called to discuss with him one by one at times depending upon his freeness and convenience.

While this system projects own style of working of such senior officer who is strict and maintains gravity always, employees will be alert and meticulous to deal with their boss who is the champion of maintaining discipline. Employees will also be very particular in maintaining timings for discussion of official matters with him, as the other employees are in the queue to meet him too. By such style of working of their boss, employees will assimilate as many points as possible to discuss with him all at a time and much time will be saved by them in not frequently meeting their superior officer for official purpose.

Maintenance of strictness and gravity are the guiding force of a competent Manager and the employees have to learn much from such officer. Employees cannot show laxity in their working before such officer because they have to work with utmost seriousness when their boss is strict and tough and maintains gravity always. Strict discipline is also generated in the employees with such tough and strict officer. Freeness in the minds of the employees is conspicuous by its absence while communing with such officer in the office. Employees also try to keep the work up-to-date as far as possible, as they are answerable to their boss if the work is kept in arear.

Q. 71. What are the ingredients in order to become potential employees?

Ans. Potential employees are the assets of Organisations. They are always in the good books of Management. Such employees are in consolidated position in employment and their rise in service is rapid. Following are the ingredients by which employees become potential:

(a) Employees have keen desire to know the unknown as far as work is concerned.

(b) They are always voracious to perform work entrusted with them.

(c) Their desire is to rise high in service by way of hard work and sincerity.

(d) They feel displeasure and restless if on any occasion they fail to attend office, which means that there is piling up of work and this may inconvenience them to keep it up-to-date.

(e) For them work is worship and they do not want to deviate from it.

(f) Punctuality in attendance to duty is their principle.

(g) They convey sense of respectability to their superiors.

(h) They do not believe in whiling away time in the office leaving the work to be done by them.

(i) They are disciplined in true sense of the term.

Q. 72. Two brothers are co-partners of an Organisation and that they often issue contradictory orders to the employees. Under the circumstances, whom should an employee carry out the orders?

Ans. Both the contradictory orders issued by the co-partners cannot be complied with by an employee. He has to carry out one of the orders. The only way out on the part of the employee is to maintain organisational discipline. He has to follow the orders from the partner in particular to whom he is reporting. But, it does not mean that the employee will outright bypass the instructions in all cases of the other partner to whom he is not reporting, especially when both the brothers are co-partners of the Organisation. It is, however, always wise that the employee should apprise of his orders to the other co-partner to whom he is directly connected as the appointing authority.

Where dissention of opinion persists in the two partners, such Organisation cannot march forward to prosperity. Employees working there cannot also think of their growth in service in such Organisation.

Q. 73. How is it essential on the part of the employees to have knowledge about the potential employers to strike the right cord?

Ans. Working system and modality of different Organisations are not the same. It depends upon the outlook and mentality of the employers in what way their Organisations are to be run. When the employees are in the know of the same, it helps them adjust, understand and perform their duties accordingly in the new environments. In this manner, they can fulfil both the expectations of the employers as well as personally satisfy themselves with the job responsibility and the job environments. When the employees work in the desired fashion of the employers rapprochement between the employees and the employers is cemented, and the right cord is struck.

Q. 74. When the male subordinate employees have their female boss in the office, how have they to work under her?

Ans. It is an admitted fact that in most of the cases male employees are not usually familiar to work under their female boss in view of the fact that the ratio of male and female bosses working in Indian offices are not balanced. At the present situation of Indian work culture, from the psychological point of view, the male subordinate employees get impetus to work sincerely and diligently especially when their female boss knows the technique of superintending in the working of the male subordinates through tender heartedness. Female bosses are by nature soft-spoken and by their sweet words the male employees feel inclined and devoted to work. This also generates sense of respectability amongst the male subordinates towards their female boss. It will not be out of place to mention here that the question of indiscipline of the male employees working under a female boss does not arise, because the employees know it very well that if indiscipline in their working is resorted to, it will be tantamount to misconduct on their part which is subject to disciplinary action.

Q. 75. How does handwriting play an important role for an employee?

Ans. Handwriting of an employee is a determinant of his personality trait and inner character. From the style of handwiring, aptitude of working of an employee is adjudged. Handwriting analysis is formally known as graphology. Graphology is a pseudo-science that claims to be a quick and easy way of reading the pulse of employees, personality and character. Many Companies in the U.S.A., France, Germany and England have resident graphologists. Through graphology they are evaluating the competence of employees. It is not unlikely that in many Indian Companies too there will be resident graphologists for the purpose of analysing the competence of the employees through graphology. Competent employees are the assets of Organisations. In most of the cases, the employees prove potential through good handwriting. It is, therefore, very important that employees should pay attention for improvement of handwriting in their own interest.

Q. 76. What are the advantages of team work of employees?

Ans. Overall efficient running of an Organisation of today does not depend upon individual performance of employees but it is the output of total working group that matters *i.e.*, overall corporate performance is a factor. It encourages cooperation amongst the co-employees. In the new dispensation, team players have the edge. Distinct advantage derived from team work is that at the instance of working in unison all employees in a department always try to maximise their efforts to be equally efficient in their working bringing prosperity to the Organisation. It also entails uniformity in the increase in the pay package of the individual employees depending upon the output of total working group. Another advantage of such uniformity in the increase in salary is that it ignites team spirit and that there is no scope for dissatisfaction in the minds of the individual employees, as there is no disuniformity in the increase in salaries of the individual employees.

Q. 77. Can an employee go on occupying Company's quarters allotted to him pending receipt of his dues in full and final settlement?

Ans. Occupation of Company's quarters by an employee beyond certain time limit after termination/leaving of his services has a criminal consequences under the provision of Section 630 of the Companies Act. The

Management can, however, consider request in writing of the ex-employee to retain the Company's quarters upto a certain extended time limit at an increased rent, as decided by them (Management). Even if the employee does not relinquish possession of the quarters within the extended time limit pending receipt of his dues, the Company can file a criminal case against the employee as per Section 630 of the Companies Act. The ex-employee should bear in mind that occupation of Company's quarters has nothing to do with the settlement of dues by the Company. It is also within the right of the ex-employee to file a case against the Company for non-payment of his dues even within the extended time limit of holding possession of the quarters by him. It is always advisable that the Company should settle his dues as early as possible but not beyond the extended time limit of holding possession of the quarters by the ex-employee.

Q. 78. What should be the job responsibilities of an Administration Assistant?

Ans. Basically, an Administration Assistant must have minimum Bachelor's Degree of any stream. He should be dynamic having strong organisational skills with the ability to handle multiple priorities and able to deal with all aspects of administrative/clerical/accounting work. He will interact with all levels of management and individual contractors which include making travel arrangements, preparing itineraries, submitting and tracking internal requests, coordinating hiring activities, meetings and group events, participate in projects, assist in preparation of presentations and correspondence, attend staff meetings, coordinate with other H.R. business partners and any other administrative work as directed by his superior official including assisting him in the discharge of his duties wherever necessary.

Q. 79. What type of criticism the employees should expect from their Managers/Senior officers when they make follies in their working?

Ans. There are two types of criticism—one is positive criticism and the other is negative criticism. Employees deserve that they are not criticised personally but their working in positive and constructive way when they are at fault. Otherwise, they will feel down-hearted and lose inspiration to work with zeal and enthusiasm. Following are the ways as to how their working with follies is to be criticised in positive and constructive manner for the purpose of heightening motivation of the employees:

(a) In the criticism there should be full of suggestions for improving the working of the employees.

(b) While criticising, opportunity has to be given to explain the position of the employees.

(c) Criticism should centre round the benefits the employees have to derive by correcting their mistakes.

(d) Criticism should be made privately and not in presence of other employees.

(e) In the criticism there should not be words of intimidation.

(f) Criticism should be made with helping attitude.

(g) Criticism should not be ambiguous so as to avoid resentment in the minds of the employees.

(h) It is the expectation of the employees that the Managers/Senior officers should be cool minded while criticising them.

Q. 80. What effects are there when the employees work under clean and peaceful atmosphere in the office?

Ans. Clean and peaceful atmosphere entice the employees falling in love with the office which in effect will improve their attendance. No employees will like to be absent from attending office unless otherwise under compelling circumstances, as they will be magnetised to the working when congeniality prevails in the office. This will also ignite enthusiasm in the minds of the employees to work with efficiency and zeal. Managers/Departmental heads have to ensure that there should not be unnecessary tension in the minds of the employees while they are at work. The employees should be kept peaceful always. If their minds are disturbed work will suffer. Hence, maintenance of clean and peaceful atmosphere is very important for increase in efficient working of the employees.

Q. 81. Should an employee join another Company with a pay-cut?

Ans. Every employee has a desire to improve his service career with consistently increase in salary. Therefore, under normal circumstances, it is foolishness to change job with lesser salary than what an employee is getting in his parent organisation. It is of course true that under certain compelling circumstances, an employee has to decide to change his company by accepting pay-cut. In the interviews the employee will be questioned about it in all his future job changes and he may be in embarrassing situation to answer to the interviewers. The employee, however, can satisfy the interviewers by telling the following reasons, as is applicable, as to why he has to accept pay-cut while changing the job:

(a) The organisation in which he is working is sinking on account of financial debilitation and as such his services are at stake.

(b) Although his salary was high there was no prospect in his employment and he would remain in the same position so long as he would be in the employ of the company.

(c) His services were transferred at a remote place where he was to have faced lot of inconveniences and accordingly his interest would have been dried up in pulling on with the job which he did not want.

(d) Working atmosphere was not congenial and peaceful and hence the company was not ideal for the prospective employee.

Employees should bear in mind that under no circumstances they should create hitch with the management during the course of employment compelling them to leave the Company and join at a lesser salary elsewhere. This will create an adverse effect on the employees, as the organisations where they would like to take up employment may in all likelihood enquire in confidence about the character and antecedents of the employees before they are issued appointment letters. Obviously, the previous employers would give bad reports about their such ex-employees.

Q. 82. Suppose, you consider yourself very expensive in terms of your fat salary you are getting from an organisation and you now have decided to leave the organisation to take up employment with other Company to expand your job horizon. In such case which is the ideal organisation for you to have change-over?

Ans. Ironically, years of experience having valuable expertise with fat salary can sometimes land you in tough situation and you may feel frustrated and discouraged when some employers are reluctant to interview you as your salary structure is the screen, because few of the employers are not willing to employ you paying high salary as it is not compatible with the salaries of their other employees of your status. In such case, when you have finally decided to switch over to other organisation for expanding your job horizon, you should try to target your job search on those organisations who pay higher than the norm for your position. These might be local offices of multinational companies or in an industry such as hi-tech firms that has to pay more to attract talent.

Q. 83. If the services of an employee, who is covered under Industrial Disputes Act, 1947, are dismissed during the period of his probation or during its extended period on the ground that the Management is not happy with his performance, the dismissed employee can of course request the concerned State Government to refer the dispute to the Industrial Tribunal and in the event of refusal to do so by the State Government what is the legal recourse left for him?

Ans. It was held by the Supreme Court that where the application of the aggrieved employee for reference of disputes to the Industrial Tribunal under the provisions of the Industrial Disputes Act is rejected by the appropriate authority *i.e.*, the State Government, the aggrieved employee can file a writ petition against the concerned authority in the High Court of the state praying for a mandatory order on the State Government to refer the dispute the employee has raised to the Industrial Tribunal. If the refusal of the authority to refer the dispute to the Industrial Tribunal is arbitrary and unreasonable, the employee is likely to succeed. In such case, the employee must not file a civil suit.

Q. 84. In an interview the interviewers may like to ask you as to why you are seeking a significant jump in salary compared to what you are getting in your present organisation. In such query what answer you have to give to satisfy them.

Ans. In the circumstances, the only way for you to say, "I chose to work at my last job for less than my market value for the very specific reasons that I wanted to glean experience of working first without taking into consideration the quantum of salary and also the employer could not afford to pay me requisite salary depending upon market value for money problem faced by them. Now, I have benefitted from experience when I look for a new prospective employer and that my market value deserves seeking a significant jump in salary befitting my talents and experience."

Q. 85. If a probationary employee takes leave on ground of exigency of circumstances during the period of his probation, will he be confirmed in his services from the next date of expiry of his probationary period/s, as mentioned in the appointment letter?

Ans. An employee is put on probation for certain months covering probationary period/s to gauge his working capability in the post in which he has been appointed and after successful completion of his probationary period/s he is confirmed in his post. When a probationary employee is not able to complete full term of his probationary period/s because of his taking leave, it will not be in order to confirm his services from the next date of completion of his probationary period/s. In such circumstances, it will be in the fitness of things to extend the date of his confirmation taking into account the number of days of leave taken by him without pay.

Q. 86. Who are workman within the purview of Industrial Disputes Act? Can their services be terminated without assigning any reason?

Ans. Section 2(d) of Industrial Disputes Act,1947 defines an employee as workman as any person employed in any business establishment to do manual, unskilled, skilled, technical, operational, clerical or supervisory work for hire or reward whether the terms of employment be express or implied. An officer can also be a workman if his working has no degree of authority involving administrative functions. Persons who are employed mainly in administrative capacity are excluded from Section 2(d) of Industrial Disputes Act, 1947.

Services of the employees who are within the purview of Section 2(d) of Industrial Disputes Act, 1947 as defined above are not to be terminated straightway without assigning any reason.

Q. 87. When the High Court of a State declares that the dismissal of an employee has become illegal directing the employer to reinstate him and the employer is not paying the full arrear salary to the employee for the period from the date of dismissal to the date of reinstatement, what step the employee can take to realise the unpaid salary?

Ans. When the order of dismissal of an employee passed by the employer has been set aside by the High Court, the reinstated employee is entitled to full arrear salary for the period from the date of dismissal to the date of reinstatement, subject to adjustment of the amounts received by him, if any. In this case, if the employer is not paying him the arrear salary, the remedy would be to file a money suit/writ petition by the employee against the employer to recover the dues. The money suit/writ petition should be filed within three years of the court order setting aside the order of dismissal by the employer.

Q. 88. If criminal charges are framed against an employee under Prevention of Corruption Act and the case is pending for disposal in the special criminal court, can the management at the same time initiate departmental proceedings against him also in the same case?

Ans. There is no taboo within the precincts of law that departmental proceedings and criminal case against a delinquent employee cannot proceed simultaneously. There was a ruling of the Supreme Court of India that departmental enquiry/proceedings could proceed simultaneously with the criminal case against the employee charged with having received illegal gratification. When an employee is charged with a criminal case, he is immediately placed under suspension and there is no escape for him from dismissal from the services of the company after the case is proved against him subsequently. Under such circumstances, management wants that such an employee is removed from the services at the soonest after the case is proved against him which may take a pretty long time after the verdict is awarded by the special criminal court. Therefore, pending receipt of the verdict of the said court, departmental proceedings will be expedited to dispose of the criminal case against the delinquent employee.

However, the Supreme Court has alternatively held that if the departmental proceedings and a criminal case are based on identical or similar set of facts and the charge in the criminal case is of a grave nature involving complicated question of law, then it is desirable to stay the departmental proceedings till the conclusion of the criminal case by the special criminal court.

Q. 89. Can the employer dispense with the services of an employee simply on the basis of a letter written to the Management by him expressing his intention to resign which might have necessitated arising out of some discord developed with the Management?

Ans. The letter of the employee addressed to the management simply speaks of the intention to resign from the services of the Organisation rather than an actual letter of resignation. Such being the situation, there is no question of acceptance of resignation of the employee by the Management. Even if the Management dispenses with the services of the employee under the circumstances mainly with the purpose of getting rid of the employee, it will be void and illegal and it can be challenged in the court of law. It is always expedient that the language, purport and context of the letter of the employee must be taken into account when interpreting the same and it has to be decided whether or not it amounts to actual resignation.

Q. 90. It is observed that in many organisations employees getting even high salaries are not still happy. What are the reasons for the same?

Ans. In certain organisations salary structure for all strata of employees is very high as compared to other organisations. Therefore, all categories of employees getting considerably high salary feel that fixation of their salary is based on the paying capacity of the organisations where they are employed. It is an axiomatic fact that in the matter of monetary benefits it is insatiable. In view of this fact and from psychological point of view, more they get more they want and hence they remain dissatisfied with the quantum of salary they receive after they are accustomed to get such high salary with the rolling of few months.

Another important factor of their dissatisfaction is that salaries of high ranking officials of the organisations are exorbitantly high and when the employees compare the quantum of their salary with that of the high ranking officials they find very big gap in the ratio of salaries which is incompatible. Under the situation, the employees feel that they are getting negligible amount of salary as compared to the high ranking officials and this leads to their unhappiness.

Q. 91. When the proceedings in the Labour Court or Industrial Tribunal may take a very long time to resolve an industrial dispute, is there any other way out of resolving such dispute expeditiously?

Ans. When there is the perception that solution of any industrial dispute may be prolonged when referred to labour court or industrial tribunal there must have alternate choice that the workmen can persuade the management to go to arbitration by mutual agreement. Section 10 of the Industrial Disputes Act provides that the employer and the workmen may agree to refer an industrial dispute to arbitration of agreed person(s). Such agreement must be in writing. The arbitrator shall investigate the dispute and submit his arbitration award to the appropriate government. On receipt of the arbitration award, the appropriate government shall then publish the award in the manner it deems fit within a month thereof and such award will be enforceable between the workmen and the management on the expiry of 30 days from the date of its publication under Section 18 of the Act. Any violation of this award by any of the parties is punishable with imprisonment for a maximum term of six months or with fine or with both.

Q. 92. After a disciplinary proceeding is initiated against an employee on allegations of misconduct, can his services be transferred to other branch of the Organisation during the currency of the disciplinary proceeding?

Ans. If it is a transferable service as per service rule and the employee does not have any legitimate grievance for his transfer unless otherwise such transfer is with malafide intention or in violation of statutory provision, there is no taboo in law in transferring services of the employee even during the currency of the disciplinary proceeding against him. The court or the tribunal cannot also interfere with such transfer orders when it is issued in the interest of administrative exigency. If, however, the employee has genuine difficulty to go on transfer he may request the Management to defer the transfer orders, when the Management may consider favourably even at the cost of administrative problem.

Q. 93. What is meant by "natural justice" and how far is it related with domestic enquiry?

Ans. The principle of natural justice has two aspects — one is that no unilateral decision should be taken by the adjudicating authority without hearing the argument of other party defending on any matter and the other is that no one can be a judge in his own cause since human instinct is to defend one's own interest.

In the disciplinary proceedings of domestic enquiry, concept of natural justice plays a vital part. Breach of natural justice in a domestic enquiry and in consequence report of the enquiry officer cannot be held good and it becomes partial and unsustainable. In such case, holding of domestic enquiry has no meaning. In this connection, it is mentioned that the court of law will not interfere in the matter even if the domestic enquiry has been conducted without adhering to the principle of natural justice, if the complaining party has not suffered in any way as a result of non-compliance with the principle of natural justice.

The defending party should of course raise objections challenging the proceedings of the domestic enquiry and report of the enquiry officer if it is conducted in violation of natural justice and the appellate authority could be informed of the same with sufficient proofs of non-compliance of natural justice. This way a domestic enquiry can be made infractuous in the event of non-adherence to natural justice.

Q. 94. Can an employee refuse to carry out reasonable orders of Management and after disobeying the same can he file a suit in the competent court of law restraining the Management to issue such orders?

Ans. In a private Organisation the relationship between an employee and the Management is based on a contract. Accordingly, refusal to carry out any lawful orders passed by the Management officials is tantamount to insubordination and a misconduct on the part of the employee, for which the employer can reasonably be expected to take disciplinary action as deemed appropriate against the employee. It is an established fact that court will not interfere in the actions of the Management except in the case of removal of an employee from the services of the Company, if the dismissal of the employee is void and illegal. Therefore, excepting in the case of wrongful dismissal, filing of suit by the employee prima facie appears to be misconceived and is likely to fail. Also the company can apply to the concerned court for quashing his suit on the ground that it is not maintainable within the precincts of law.

Q. 95. If any Management desists from clearance of all dues payable to an ex-employee quitting employment of an Organisation, what is the course left for him to get all his unpaid money from the Management?

Ans. In the event of non-receipt of dues after termination of employment remedy lies with the ex-employee that he has to execute the decree in accordance with the provisions of the Code of Civil Procedure, 1908. An execution application will have to be accompanied by a certified copy of the decree, duly obtained from the Decree Department of the High Court and then he will file an execution application in the said court. In this connection, it is to be noted that under Section-87 of the Civil Procedure Code, execution shall not be issued on any decree against the organisation unless the decree remains unsatisfied for at least three months from the date of the decree.

Q. 96. If the employer fails to pay the E.S.I. contributions; what is the way out to recover the same?

Ans. If an Organisation fails to pay the E.S.I. contributions, the aggrieved employee/s can lodge complaint with the authorised officer (defined under Section 45 of the Act), who may issue to the recovery officer a certificate specifying the amount of arrears payable by the defaulting organisation. The recovery officer shall then proceed to recover the certified amount from the defaulting employer *inter alia* by attachment and sale of the employer's movable and immovable properties or by other methods as specified in Section 45(C) of the Act.

Q. 97. When the Management levels some false allegations with some malicious intent against an employee having unblemished service record for a number of years, and suspending him from service and in the event of exoneration from all the charges during the course of enquiry proceedings, can the employee file a suit for recovery of damages for the loss of reputation from the Management?

Ans. If the departmental proceedings go in favour of the employee and ultimately he is exonerated from the charges framed against him with some malicious intent or the other, he is bound to be reinstated with all back arrears and benefits which were withdrawn during the period of suspension. Once the employee is in a position to clearly establish that the proceedings were in fact initiated and conducted without just cause or sufficient cause and with malicious intent, he is entitled to seek further compensation for the humiliation he had suffered for which he can file a suit for recovery of damages for loss of reputation. Admittedly, such cases are not filed, if the employees wants to remain in peaceful employment with the employer. But, at the same time it is suggested that when the employer has tried to implicate the employee by levelling false charges against him with the clear intention to get rid of him from the services of the Organisation, he should not continue with the Organisation in his own interest and should of course file suit against the employer for recovery of damages for loss of reputation suffered by him.

Q. 98. How could the sweet and cordial employee-employer relations help forging ahead of an Organisation towards prosperity as also the employees?

Ans. Sweet and cordial relations benefit both the employees and the employer. Employees tend to have inclination to work for the Organisation with zeal, enthusiasm and energy treating it as their own which leads to attainment of efficiency in the running of the Organisation when the Management recognises the services of the employees. Employees also devote to full attention to the working after they are satisfied in the matter of fixation of proper salary/wages and other fringe benefits enabling them to work with free mind and without thinking of financial stringency. While the employees and the employer should work shoulder to shoulder for the purpose of maintaining sweet and cordial relations between them, the Management should also see that congenial working atmosphere is maintained in the Organisation. This will help the employees to work with full devotion which in turn efficiency in the working of the employees will be augmented. By such efficient working of the employees the Organisation forges ahead of prosperity and the employees grow up with the growth of the Organisation. Troubled Organisation is a sign of degeneration which can be arrested by maintaining sweet relation with the employees. Therefore, sweet and cordial employee-employer relations are the essence of benefits for both the employees and the employer.

Q. 99. How are the work culture and motivation important for an employee?

Ans. Without motivation work culture of an employee cannot be improved upon. Motivation induces an employee to keep himself busy in his job. Motivation is an excitement or inducement to action. In other words, motivation means an inclination to work and this inclination to work breeds work culture. In the office it is very often observed that some of the employees are not serious in their working. This is due to lack of motivation. Employees are motivated or induced to work when there is encouragement from the Management officials and this plays a very important role. After motivating the employees and rewarding them from time to time for the commendable job done, the employees will tend to work with full devotion which will result in attaining their efficiency and this efficiency will ultimately prove effective for getting promotion. Hence, there is relativity between the words, motivation and work culture. Improvement in work culture amongst the employees means efficient running of the Organisation. Also by the work culture attendance to office will improve and the employees will feel responsibility to the job assigned to them.

Q.100. What should the employees give preference—salary or employment?

Ans. It is an admitted fact that salary and employment are relative. Money is of course a criterion for every employee to keep his body and soul together which is possible when he gets salary/remuneration in return of services rendered by him to the Organisation where he is employed. The only difference is that the quantum of salary/remuneration differs from Organisation to Organisation. If an employee attaches much importance to his remuneration in preference to his employment, it will only exhibit that he is very much voracious and the work he does is of less importance to him. This is like putting the cart before the horse and not the horse before the cart. Every ambitious employee has to bear in mind that if he is devoted to work whole-heartedly he is destined to attain prosperity in service today or tomorrow and he will be rewarded suitably by way of fixation of his salary commensurate to his exalted position. Hence, the question of salary should not be given upper hand but the way he works for the Organisation for fulfilling the expectation of the higher Management which will be ultimately advantageous to him after he gets exalted position in service with increased salary.

